Philosophy for Teens

Philosophy
FOR TEENS

Core Concepts and Life's Biggest Questions Examined

MARK LINSENMAYER

**ROCKRIDGE
PRESS**

First Rockridge Press trade paperback edition 2022

Rockridge Press and the Rockridge Press logo are trademarks or registered trademarks of Callisto Media Inc. and/or its affiliates in the United States and other countries and may not be used without written permission.

For general information on our other products and services, please contact our Customer Care Department within the United States at (866) 744-2665, or outside the United States at (510) 253-0500.

Paperback ISBN: 978-1-63878-231-5 | ebook ISBN: 978-1-63878-286-5

Manufactured in the United States of America

Interior and Cover Designer: Erik Jacobsen
Art Producer: Melissa Malinowsky
Editor: Barbara J. Isenberg
Production Editor: Cassie Gitkin
Production Manager: Martin Worthington

Illustration © 2022 Amy Blackwell, pp. 2, 5, 15, 32, 39, 66, 84, 112, 121, 130; iStock, cover; All other illustrations used under license from Shutterstock.com

Author photo courtesy of Josh Casey

10 9 8 7 6 5 4 3 2 1 0

THIS BOOK IS FOR
KIM, ABE, AND MINA.

Contents

Introduction

Welcome to philosophy, where you'll learn a lot of fun ideas that just might help you think more clearly and creatively.

A long time ago, when I was a teen, a friend of mine pointed out to me that in the conversations I was having with him about what we believed in and what made the most sense to do with our lives, I was already doing philosophy. Before then, I'd been interested in figuring things out, but I hadn't connected this to actually studying philosophy. Why should I care about what people hundreds or even thousands of years ago thought?

But as I studied more, I became fascinated with the history of thought. I came to appreciate how incredibly lucky we are to have so many texts passed down from ancient times (remember, people had to copy these by hand to preserve them) and how many wild and wonderful things philosophers are still working on today.

I studied philosophy in school for eight years, then quit that to get a "real job" for a while, but I just couldn't keep away from philosophy. I've now been running a philosophy reading group podcast called *The Partially Examined Life* for over a decade. Each new idea gets my mind racing, and I'm so happy that I get to share those ideas with my audience, which now includes you.

In this book you'll meet some really interesting characters and theories that I've come across over the years, from a thinker named Thales who declared that everything is water to another called Nagarjuna who claimed that everything is really nothing. We'll talk about intelligent computers, whether horror movies can be beautiful, and ways that an argument can crash and burn.

This book presents philosophy through questions that you might have asked yourself, like: Can we prove the existence of a God? What are minds, really? Are there some things we just can't know for sure?

I will also try to show you how to break down questions into smaller ones. So I don't just ask, What are right and wrong? Instead, you'll see five different questions that get at different aspects of this.

The point is to help you think and talk more clearly about these issues. That way, when you disagree with someone, you can figure out exactly what you disagree about. Many disagreements just come from not seeing a problem in the same way.

For example, I really like music: I listen to it all the time, and I write songs. People disagree about what good music is. Asking questions about how musical taste works has helped me be open to new kinds of music that I previously never saw the point of. This has opened me up to the *people* who like that music. I can understand and get along with them better.

Ideas are a lot like music: By learning more about ideas, you can get along better with people who think differently from you. You'll find that many of these philosophers think differently from anyone you've ever met. This book is structured so you can skip around to parts that seem most interesting to you, and if you see an unfamiliar word or name, just flip to the back to the Glossary or Philosopher Guide.

Let's get started!

CHAPTER 1

All About Philosophy: Why Ask Why?

L et's start off by getting clear about what kinds of things you'll be reading about in this book. What is philosophy, and how is it different from science or religion or anything else? Why should you be interested in what philosophers have to say? Why should you become a philosopher yourself?

THE HISTORY OF PHILOSOPHY

The word "philosophy" is actually two Greek words stuck together: The *philo-* part means "love of," or (since all translations are approximate) "liking," and the *-sophy* part is from *sophia*, which means "wisdom," or maybe "intelligence," or "cleverness," or "skill."

So philosophy is the love of wisdom, or at least liking being smart. Importantly, it's not *being* wise or smart or clever. It's *wanting* to be those things.

Everybody likes an origin story, like when a superhero gets bitten by something radioactive or loses a loved one and because of that vows to fight for a better world.

Philosophy has a story like that. Back around 400 BCE, there was this fellow in Athens, Greece, named **Socrates** who used to go around asking important people why they believed the things they did. Inevitably, Socrates would show that these very important people really didn't know what they were talking about. They didn't like this, and so they accused Socrates of irreverence to the gods and corrupting young people. Socrates was convicted and sentenced to death.

Carrying out the sentence, Socrates drank the poison. He knew that he'd done nothing wrong, but he'd lived a good life, and if this was the verdict of his city, then so be it.

Inspired by Socrates, his student **Plato** wrote down all the stories he knew about his teacher, since Socrates had never written any books himself. Plato's books remain the most read works of philosophy today, and all the philosophers who have come after him are either responding to him or responding to others' responses to him. Essentially, Plato started a conversation that we're still having.

Plato's students founded a number of distinct schools emphasizing different aspects of his thought, and these splintered and influenced and spread around the world, with the Islamic world preserving Greek texts after the fall of the Roman Empire and religious leaders of the Middle Ages transforming Greek thought into Christian (and Jewish and Islamic) doctrine. In the Renaissance (around the 14th century), many Greek and Roman texts were rediscovered in Europe, and this kicked off the Enlightenment, which included the birth of science and all those famous philosophers like René Descartes, John Locke, and Immanuel Kant.

Post-Kant, there was a divergence between analytic philosophy—centered in England and America and highly influenced by mathematics and the effort to make philosophy more scientific—and continental philosophy—centered in France and Germany and open to more sprawling, poetic writing. These are informal categories of philosophy, and there are many philosophers who don't fit into either category or reject this division altogether.

And of course systematic thought didn't start only in Greece. India and China, in particular, have ancient philosophical traditions, and Western philosophers have only recently, and in fits and starts, really started incorporating their insights, as well as philosophy from Africa, Indigenous Americans, and many other groups, into mainstream philosophical thought. With the information explosion that is the internet, the field of philosophy is more fragmented than ever. This book aims to give you a starting point to explore more on your own.

THE BRANCHES OF PHILOSOPHY

Philosophy is not just one area of study. It's the beginning of all questioning, and different branches of it focus on different topics. Let's preview the areas that you'll be reading about in this book.

METAPHYSICS: WHAT IS REALITY?

Metaphysics asks questions about what the world is really like. The core of metaphysics is **ontology**, which is the study of being and of what it is to exist. Philosophers try to make a list of which types of things they think really exist. Probably unicorns shouldn't be on the list. But what about **souls**? What about any higher power? Maybe a god is actually the only real thing, and we're all just ideas in this god's mind. Maybe only tiny atomic particles should be on the list, because everything else is just built out of them.

Metaphysicians also look at how things fit together: How parts make wholes, how new things grow out of old things, and how one event makes another happen. For instance: How do minds exist in a physical world?

Some metaphysical questions overlap with science, especially physics, which is the study of the physical world. "Meta" is a prefix that has to do with studying the foundations of something, of turning the questioning back on that thing.

A physicist might study how physical things interact, like how much damage a car will take when it hits a concrete wall at 80 miles per hour. Metaphysics asks more general, underlying questions: What is motion? What is it for two things to interact? What is it to be a thing at all?

EPISTEMOLOGY: WHAT CAN WE KNOW?

In studying metaphysics, you might have asked, "How would I know what's ultimately real and what's not?"

Epistemology, the study of knowledge, is your central place for answering this and many other questions. "Episteme" means knowledge in Greek. How can you actually be sure that this book isn't lying to you? How can you be sure that you're actually reading a book right now? It sure seems like you are, but maybe you're dreaming. Maybe you think you're in a chair reading, but you're really in a pod filled with goo hooked up to a computer simulation that's making you *think* you're in a chair.

Realistically, you don't have to worry about being in this type of scenario. But asking what seem like obvious questions—such as How do I know I'm really holding a book?—helps us answer some difficult, more general questions: What counts as evidence that something is true? What does "truth" even mean? Is any of our knowledge ever really *certain*, and if it isn't, so what?

Science takes itself to be the enterprise that's here to figure out what we should believe, but is that warranted? What kinds of claims can science legitimately make? Which questions count as scientific ones? Are there some areas where science needs to just butt out?

ETHICS: WHAT ARE WE SUPPOSED TO DO?

Ethics asks questions about what you should do and what kind of person you want to be. What is right and wrong?

A code of ethics can just be a list of rules to follow or maybe just a single, fundamental rule like "Treat others as you want to be treated." But the study of ethics is not just about which code is the right one, but whether there's a right one at all.

If an adult in your life tells you that you should be nice to your brother, what does the word "should" really mean? Does it just mean they *want* you to be nice? Is talking about ethics just like booing or cheering at a game? If you boo at a football game, you're not really commenting on the players' skills. You're just expressing your feelings about them. Are claims about ethics just expressions of what someone wants or likes? Or are there really rules that are objectively right, so that your mother is not just stating her opinion but saying something *true* when she says you should be nice?

In addition to exploring moral rules, ethics also includes ethical psychology, which looks at what motivates people to do the right thing. One metaphysical question that has profound effects on ethics is free will: Are we really free to choose our actions?

Some of the philosophers we'll be discussing in this area include Confucius, Laozi, Plato, Aristotle, Epictetus, Augustine, Jeremy Bentham, Immanuel Kant, John Stuart Mill, and Friedrich Nietzsche.

LOGIC: WHAT'S A GOOD ARGUMENT?

Logic is your tool kit for trying to figure out and prove how various claims in philosophy relate to other claims. (A "claim" is just a sentence that someone is saying is true.)

Logicians have developed symbols to help us understand how **arguments** work. You probably studied algebra, where x is a variable that stands for any number. In symbolic logic, you can represent a claim with a capital letter like P.

If you want to argue that believing P is a good reason for also believing Q, you can express that is as "If P is true, then Q is true," which can be shortened to $P \rightarrow Q$. This kind of shorthand is useful for allowing us to see argument structures.

Of course, when you're arguing, you're not going to stop and do some math. But studying logic will help you be clear about what you really mean, and it will give you the power to spot bad arguments and say exactly what's wrong with them.

In this book, I'll expose you to some different ways that logicians have symbolized arguments, and talk about how logicians have contributed to scientific thinking (epistemology) and arguments in ethics. You'll also learn some **informal fallacies**, which are typically mistakes that make it impossible to adequately translate an ordinary argument into logical symbols.

AESTHETICS: WHAT IS GOOD ART?

The word "**aesthetics**" refers to the study of the beautiful. What makes an artwork or a landscape you'd see out your window beautiful (or not)? Are there measurable properties, such as symmetry, in beautiful objects that give us pleasure?

Beauty isn't the only quality that can make art good. A movie could be great because it's scary, or thought provoking. Some kinds of music—like death metal—don't aim for beauty: They want to be intense. You might find someone's appearance to be really appealing, even "striking," even if it's not what you think society would call beautiful.

To capture all this, some philosophers like the term "philosophy of art" instead of aesthetics. Whatever term you use, our concern here is people's tastes: Why do we like (and dislike) the things we do?

You may think tastes are just personal. You like what you like, and I like what I like, and that's all there is to say about it. Neither of us is wrong. This seems like a polite point of view, because no one is being arrogant enough to claim that their tastes are better than someone else's. But when we're talking about how great an artwork is, aren't we saying more than just "I like it"? We're talking about the art, not about ourselves.

POLITICAL PHILOSOPHY: WHAT KIND OF GOVERNMENT SHOULD WE HAVE?

Political philosophy deals with how we should live together. What kind of society do we want, and how should it be governed? What qualities should a good political leader have?

We all want to live in peace, but peace could involve a tyrant *forcing* us all to be peaceful. Is that what we want, or do we also need freedom and justice? What do these terms really mean? Are we free just because the government leaves us alone, or is real freedom the ability—the power—to live the way we really want?

Political philosophy lives next door to ethics. In ethics, we ask what we should do as individuals. In political philosophy, we ask what we should do as a group. What laws should we pass, and how should our government treat its citizens? When people disagree about something really important, who gets to resolve the dispute?

One interesting area within political philosophy has to do with how the economy—our system of wealth and jobs—should interact with our government. Should the economy just be free to spin along, or is it a tool the government can use to take care of people? Is it even the job of government to take care of people at all?

ASKING QUESTIONS

Wondering about things is what keeps our brains alive. You should never feel like you have it all figured out and can stop being curious.

Most questions have definite answers: How do bees make honey? How does my phone work? How does a bill become a law? Questions in philosophy are different. You can't just do a web search to get an answer. You can't just ask an expert. A philosophical question is one that *you* have to answer yourself, using your very own brain.

Every philosophical question is open-ended. This means there are always new possible answers. Even if it looks like a yes-or-no question, the reasoning might be different, or your answer might be "Yes, but . . . " and what comes after "but" is your own thought. For instance, "Is there a God?" seems like a question for which there should be a yes-or-no answer. But your reasons for believing or not believing will be your own, and there are many different ideas about what exactly the word "God" refers to.

The best philosophical questions are important and personal. What's the point of getting up in the morning? How can I love someone fully? What kind of world do we want to live in?

Now, you may find that some of the questions in this book don't seem that way to you, and that's okay. Maybe you're not too concerned about why people find some things beautiful, or what standards scientists use to decide when to switch to a new theory. But for some people, these are vital, central questions in their lives, and by studying these questions, you may understand those people better.

For some philosophical questions, it's not obvious why anyone would care about them. For example, do numbers, or properties like "red" and "soft," or possibilities for the future actually exist? You may not understand why those are even questions at all.

There's usually a practical upshot to even the most abstract-sounding questions. The previous questions are about existence, something that we should all be very concerned about, because caring about something that doesn't actually exist wouldn't make much sense, would it? So it matters what existence is and which things really exist.

In this book, you'll learn about structuring arguments, how new ideas develop, and how minor differences between ideas can have big implications. Studying philosophy is great if you're interested in being a lawyer, going into politics, or writing profound books. But I also want you to try to shake off the idea that everything worth doing has to have a practical application. Many mathematicians love what they do just because the play of numbers and concepts they work with is beautiful. I hope to give you a hint of why I think this is true of philosophical concepts, too.

Reading philosophy isn't only for people who want to be professional philosophers. It's just a fun, challenging, and joyful thing that we're lucky enough to get to do.

CHAPTER 2

Metaphysics: What Is Reality?

Any question about the makeup of the world is a metaphysical one. This is the area that has the most overlap with science. In fact, scientists used to be called "natural philosophers." Metaphysics, though, can ask questions that are more basic than the ones science asks. But both metaphysics and science can reveal that reality is very different from what we normally think it is.

WHAT IS REALITY?

What does it mean for something to be real, to actually exist? This question might seem very easy. We deal with things we believe are real—people, chairs, phones—all day.

However, sometimes we see illusions. When you look at a rainbow, it looks like there's a giant arc of colored glass in the sky, but there isn't. Is it possible that people, chairs, and phones are really illusory as well?

One reason to consider this possibility is that we know that rainbows are really just moisture particles in the air refracting and reflecting sunlight. The particles are real, but the rainbow isn't.

Well, aren't all ordinary objects also made of particles? Maybe *every* time we see something, we're being fooled. The tiny, invisible particles are what's truly real, and the objects we see are not.

To decide whether this could be true, we have to better understand what we mean by "reality."

WHO ASKED IT?

The Upanishads were scriptures written in India between 800 and 300 BCE as part of a larger set of scriptures called the Vedas. The unknown authors of the Upanishads asked what is truly real, and their answer was Brahman. They defined "Brahman" as unchanging and eternal yet conscious stuff that underlies and causes all visible things.

If Brahman is all that is truly real, what about those visible things? They're illusory, and yet we treat them as real, and with good reason! We couldn't get along in the world if we didn't treat our food, loved ones, and other things as real.

WHO ANSWERED IT?

Plato agreed that the things we see are less real than divine things. Instead of Brahman, Plato believed in a transcendent (beyond the normal world) realm of Forms. **Platonic Forms** are perfect models of the things we see on Earth.

For example, if you see a dog, you're actually using a Dog Form to recognize that dog. The Form is what makes it a dog.

The dog you are seeing is just an imperfect, less real copy of the Form.

The more commonly used name for a general concept like "dog" is a *universal*. A universal concept groups together different things, and lots of philosophers have wondered whether universals are actually real (like Platonic Forms) or just mental tools that we use to classify things.

The 13th-century English friar **William of Occam** (sometimes spelled Ockham), unlike Plato, was not a *realist* about universals. Instead, he was a *nominalist*. *Nom* is the Latin word for "name," and a nominalist says that a word is just a name that doesn't name anything in reality.

I bet you're a nominalist about Santa Claus. That name doesn't refer to anyone in reality, but because of the many stories about Santa Claus, we can talk about him: he has a beard, does not have three eyes, and so on. You might say that he's a real work of fiction.

If something exists only nominally, then we should be able to explain how it appears out of the actions by things or people that are real. We can explain the illusion.

In Real Life

Is money real? Of course we think paper and coins are real. But is their value—the *concept* of money—real?

This question is about social construction, about things that are only real because we say so. Money is only valuable if the people exchanging it believe it is. If a government were to collapse, then the paper bills and coins that government produced might become worthless.

Some philosophers have argued that anything that is potentially fleeting can't truly be real in the first place. There's something unreal about money, status, and the other things that we just "make up."

Taking Sides

One useful idea for debating reality is reductionism. If you think something (like money, the universal concept "dog," or the whole visible world) isn't truly real, this means it can be reduced, or redescribed, by talking only about things that you do think are real.

A materialist is someone who thinks that only matter is ultimately real. The 17th-century English philosopher Thomas Hobbes argued that there's no such thing as a soul, only a mind, which is really just a body doing certain things. In other words, the soul is reducible to matter.

Brahman in the Upanishads, on the other hand, is a spiritual, conscious "God-stuff." Individual human souls and matter are different substances, but both are somehow reducible to Brahman.

If ordinary objects are real in a way that rainbows are not, that means they aren't reducible at all, whether to atoms or to ideas of God.

Consider This

- Do you think everything is either real or not real? Or are there *degrees* of being real, so that things can be *sort of* real?

- Is there more than one kind of reality? For example, are subatomic particles real in one way, while ordinary objects are real in another way?

WHAT KINDS OF THINGS REALLY EXIST?

An ontology is a list of basic sorts of things that exist. Our everyday ontology includes everyday physical objects, but as we just discussed, maybe these are only nominally and not ultimately real.

What are the ultimate elements of reality? Is reality ultimately just one big thing (like God), or many tiny things? Or maybe it's not a "thing" at all: Some philosophers have argued that it's actually an event (a happening) instead, or that it's nothing at all. Finally, some philosophers have argued that this is a totally meaningless question, that there's no "ultimate" existence at all.

WHO ASKED IT?

Thales of Miletus (a city in what is now Turkey) was considered by ancient Greeks to have been the first philosopher. He lived a couple hundred years before Socrates, and history has not preserved any of his books, just quotations from them in works by later writers.

Thales came up with the idea that even though all the things in nature around us look very different from each other, maybe they're all really made of a single kind of stuff: water. All things come into being from water, and eventually turn back into water.

WHO ANSWERED IT?

Other early philosophers around Greece came up with their own versions of a primary metaphysical principle: a single stuff or force that constitutes the world. **Anaximenes of Miletus** argued that maybe the world is not all water, but instead air. **Anaxagoras** said maybe it's all a vast, cosmic mind. **Heraclitus** said that there is no ultimate, unchanging reality at all; instead, there is only change. **Democritus** is credited with coming up with the idea that everything is made up of many tiny indivisible atoms.

Aristotle, the most famous student of Plato, said there's not one basic type of stuff at all. Instead, he came up with eleven basic categories of existence. He called individual objects (like a dog) "substances," which have various qualities (like brown and furry), are in relation to other things, stand in a certain spatial position, etc. The idea is that the parts of speech (nouns, verbs, adjectives, etc.) each pick out different fundamental elements of the world.

Still, Aristotle considered substance the most real of the categories. Qualities and actions and such all need a substance; there's no "brown" by itself, but only brown dogs, brown bricks, etc. But substances are independent and fundamental.

The Buddhist philosopher **Nagarjuna** (circa 200 CE) denied that anything was independent and described reality as emptiness. Everything relies on something else for its being, with no ultimate foundation. There is no underlying God, Brahman, or Forms to give everything reality, so it's all ultimately an illusion.

In Real Life

Heraclitus expressed his idea that everything is change by saying, "You never step in the same river twice."

What is a river? It's flowing water, so the water molecules you step in once will be long gone by the time you come back.

Heraclitus clarified: It's not just the river that will be different when you come back—*you* will be different as well. We're all constantly changing, and everything that we might try to examine using philosophy is constantly changing, too.

This makes doing philosophy difficult; it's like what we're trying to study is just constantly slipping out from under us.

Taking Sides

The early-20th-century **Austrian British philosopher Ludwig Wittgenstein** was exceptional for changing his whole philosophical approach.

In his early work, he argued that the basic elements of existence are not things or basic categories, but facts. A fact is a connection between a thing and a property, such as "the dog is brown." He claimed that all the complex facts of our world are built out of basic atomic facts.

However, in his later work, Wittgenstein rejected all metaphysics. He argued that all speech—including philosophy—makes use of social contexts that he called "language games." If you're playing the physics game, you might need to refer to atoms. If you're playing the grammar game, you'd refer to nouns, adjectives, etc. So a game can include an ontology—a list of things needed to play the game—but we can't say anything about the world outside the game.

Consider This

- Do you agree with Heraclitus that everything is change? Or do you agree with Plato that reality is ultimately changeless?

- Could a quality like "brown" be reducible to substances, like little particles of light bouncing off objects and hitting our eyes?

HOW DOES ONE THING CAUSE ANOTHER?

When one ball on a pool table hits another, making it roll toward the corner pocket, what's really going on? All we actually see are the movements of the two balls, one happening after the other in a predictable way.

Correlation is when two things tend to appear (and increase or decrease) together. People who are driving cars tend to also be people who are wearing clothes, but it's not like driving causes someone to wear clothes.

So what is it about **causality**—when one event actually produces another—that makes it more than just correlation? This concept is central to science, and to how we make sense of the world.

WHO ASKED IT?

Ancient India's traditional Hindu view that everything is Brahman made causality very puzzling. If we only have one thing in our ontology, then causality just can't be real at all, because two things are required: a cause and an effect.

However, another part of Hinduism (and Buddhism) is reincarnation. People's actions *cause* them to be reborn repeatedly to new lives according to a law of **karma**.

If causality is just part of conventional reality—illusions that we all agree on out of convenience—then how could Brahman *cause* the various parts of conventional reality to exist?

WHO ANSWERED IT?

The Samkhya school in India (started around 350 CE by **Ishvarakrisna**) claimed that the one true reality must have all its effects already in it, so causality never actually produces anything new. It's just the appearance of something that was already really there.

According to **Siddhartha Gautama** (also known as the Buddha), the world has no underlying reality at all. Instead, each existing thing is only momentary. The Buddhist philosopher Nagarjuna extended this idea to argue that our ordinary understanding of causality is based on faulty ideas that cause and effect are independent from each other and from our minds.

Aristotle thought causality was real, and he identified four ways that we can talk about it. Something is caused by prior events (its efficient cause), but also by the material that it's made of, its form, and its purpose (final cause). For example, a house is caused by the people who build it, but also by the wood, nails, etc., from which it's made, the way that these are arranged to make the house, and the blueprint with the directions followed to build it.

The Persian theologian **Abu Hamid al-Ghazali** argued that causality involves necessity: If the cause happens, then the effect *has to* happen. But he also argued that only God can necessarily make anything happen, so only God can be a cause.

The 18th-century Scottish philosopher **David Hume** thought causality was just one event happening after another, plus our *expectation* that it will always happen that way.

In Real Life

Sometimes we think of causation as involving an object exerting a power on another object. Does scientific thinking require this? No! Science is about finding regularities in nature, so Hume's description of causation as nothing but a *pattern* within events is all we need.

Think about the law of gravity. We often talk about gravity *causing* things to fall, but we really don't know why they fall. Physics only tells us that objects attract each other in predictable ways, so we can say how fast something will fall, how planets move, how a spaceship can break orbit, etc.

Taking Sides

The French priest **Nicolas Malebranche** (like al-Ghazali) thought the only *true* cause was God. It might look like *I* hit the cue ball that knocked the eight ball into the corner pocket, but the cause is always actually God.

Of course, I still get credit for getting the ball in; it's not like we declare God the winner (and loser!) of every game. According to Malebranche, my action created an *occasion* for God to cause something to happen.

Occam's razor, a principle that says to look for the simplest explanation, suggests that we therefore don't *need* to talk about God as a cause at all. But Malebranche had metaphysical reasons for insisting that we do. He didn't think that matter (substance) was the kind of thing that could actually *do* anything at all.

Aristotle, by contrast, had a very different view of substance that allows it to be causal in multiple ways.

Consider This

- Try to list as many causes as you can of you reading this book right now. What kinds of causes come to mind?

- What do you think *substance* is? If you take away all the qualities something has (its color, texture, smell, etc.), what would be left?

CAN WE PROVE THE EXISTENCE OF A GOD?

Whether there is a God affects lots of other metaphysical questions. Consequently, many philosophers have constructed proofs of the existence of a Supreme Being. They wanted to show beyond any doubt that God exists.

This is complicated by the different definitions and qualities that different traditions and philosophers might use to describe a Supreme Being. A common definition that philosophers start with in trying to construct a proof for God's existence is that God is a being that is everywhere (omnipresent), knows everything (omniscient), and is all-powerful (omnipotent) and perfect in every way.

WHO ASKED IT?

The Hindu tradition posed the question this way: If everything is Brahman, then how can there be just one part of that stuff—a creator God—that made the rest of it?

A lot of ancient Indian philosophy consists of commentary on scriptures and on earlier commentaries. The 8th-century CE philosopher **Shankara** analyzed a much older collection of texts called the Brahma-sutra to come up with an argument for the existence of a creator God (using the Sanskrit word "Isvara" instead of "Brahman"). The world looks designed—like a piece of pottery—therefore, it must have had a designer.

WHO ANSWERED IT?

Shankara's argument was an early version of what philoso-phers call "the argument from design." You may have heard the formulation from 1,000 years later by British clergy-man **William Paley**: If you found a watch on the beach, you wouldn't think it just grew there, right? It must have had a maker. The world, with all its complexity, must also have a maker.

The 12th-century monk **Anselm of Canterbury** came up with an argument that relies on God being the most per-fect possible being. This would mean God has all the best qualities, in the highest degree. Do you think *existing* is a good quality? Anselm argued that it is better to exist than not exist. Therefore God, by definition, has that property: God exists.

In 10th-century Iran, the philosopher-scientist **Ibn Sina** (also known as Avicenna) gave a version of Aristotle's cos-mological argument, which looks at the chain of causality we observe in the world to posit a prime mover: something that got causality itself started. In Ibn Sina's version, the chain is not causality in time (the physical chain of causes goes on forever) but a chain of dependence. Everything depends on something else for its existence, so there must be some foun-dational entity that everything else depends on.

Around 1800, the German philosopher **Immanuel Kant** argued that we can't prove God's existence at all, because metaphysics is beyond human knowledge. Instead, we have to have **faith**—like the fact that bad things happen to good people—in order for the world to make sense to us.

In Real Life

The problem of evil is an argument against God's existence that goes back to 300 BCE and the Greek philosopher Epicurus. If God is good and all-powerful, then God could prevent tragedy, yet terrible things happen to good people. Therefore, there can't be a God.

Think about natural disasters that kill millions: plagues, famines, floods, erupting volcanoes, and other calamities. Many of these are in no way a result of human choices. They're just part of life. Why would a good God create life in this way? How could a good God allow people to suffer so much?

Taking Sides

Aristotle and his admirer Ibn Sina reached different conclusions about causality. Aristotle described causality as a long chain of cause and effect. If there weren't a first cause, then the whole process couldn't have gotten moving at all.

Ibn Sina didn't see any absurdity in an infinitely long chain of events in time, so long as the whole chain was divinely supported somehow. God exists not as an event within time, but as the source of all time (and everything else).

So who's right? Immanuel Kant argued that we have no way of deciding this. Our idea of causality only applies to finite things in experience. We have no justification for making any larger cosmic judgments about it. The same logic goes for any other arguments about God. We can only prove things based on principles of reason (like mathematics) or things we experience. Belief in God requires faith.

Consider This

- What do you think about the definition of God given at the beginning of this question?

- Are you convinced by any of the arguments for God's existence?

- Try to respond to the problem of evil: Can you explain why a good God would allow evil to exist?

WHAT ARE MINDS?

Each of us has an inner life: a stream of conscious experiences that you can't put into words, that no one else can sense but you.

How does consciousness fit into a world that looks material? For science to study something, we have to be able to measure it. It has to be observable by multiple scientists so that they can repeat each other's experiments. But while a scientist could look at your brain activity, no one can see your mind—your own conscious experiences—but you.

Do our minds exist? Or are minds somehow reducible to just brains?

WHO ASKED IT?

Again, let's start with India, with that view that Brahman is everything, and that it is conscious (think of it as "God-stuff"). Everything is one big mind. Yet it doesn't seem this way. We see what looks like dead matter all around us.

The Samkhya school responded with the theory that this single divine world has two ways of appearing to us: *prakriti*, which is basic material stuff, and *purusha*, spirit or consciousness.

The 17th-century Dutch philosopher **Baruch Spinoza** also argued that there's only one fundamental kind of stuff in the universe, yet it has a mental aspect and a physical aspect.

Many philosophers were motivated by religious concerns to ask about the relation between the mental and the physical. If the mind is somehow identical to the body (or more cosmically, if mind and body are both aspects of a single underlying world), then when a body dies, its mind must die, too.

Plato asked this question in his **dialogue** *Phaedo*, which depicted Socrates right before his death. He argued that there must be something that makes dead matter alive. This is life itself, and in our case, that means our conscious mind. How could life itself die? Therefore, our minds (our souls) must survive after the body dies.

WHO ANSWERED IT?

The 17th-century French philosopher **René Descartes** argued for metaphysical **dualism**, the view that mind and body are fundamentally different substances. He thought this because of our very different ways of accessing these things. I only know about material things in the world through my senses, which can be fooled (like when I am seeing a rainbow). I know about my mind from the inside; I can't be mistaken about the things I "see" that way.

An early version of this argument by Ibn Sina asks you to picture yourself floating, with your limbs spread out so you can't feel any part of them. Your eyes are closed, your ears and nose are stopped up, and you have no memory, so you have no sensation at all, no knowledge of the outside world. Yet even then, you would know that you exist. Therefore the soul (this inner you that you know) must be different from the body and the rest of the world.

If mind and body are fundamentally different substances, then how could they possibly interact? A different kind of dualism that avoids this problem is **functionalism**. Instead of thinking about mind as a substance that is different from body, let's think about it as an *activity* that the body does, as a *function* of the body.

An early functionalist was Descartes's English contemporary Thomas Hobbes. According to Hobbes, thinking is just matter moving according to mathematical principles. Modern computer scientists who think machines can be made to think are using this functionalist idea. A thinking computer is just one whose material parts are organized in the right way. Its hardware is like a human brain, and its software is like the pattern of neurons firing in the brain. In 1950, computer scientist **Alan Turing** suggested that if a computer could fool a human into thinking it is intelligent, then we're justified in actually calling it intelligent: This is known as the Turing test.

One famous response to functionalism is American philosopher **Thomas Nagel**'s 1974 article "What Is It Like to Be a Bat?" Nagel argues that the essential thing about being a mind is consciousness. Even a bat has its own stream of experiences, ones that we can't imagine (since we don't use echolocation like bats do). Even if a computer imitates a mind, it's not actually a mind unless it's conscious. Can running the right program make a machine conscious?

In Real Life

Robots that seem intelligent are still just science fiction for now, but maybe not for long. When a robot becomes sophisticated enough to report on its own states, to ask questions and ponder the answers, to become concerned that it might not have a real soul, does that mean we should start to treat it like a person? Will it gain political rights and moral responsibilities?

Would you insist, like Nagel, that such a machine still has no conscious experience, that it is just an imitation mind, not a real one?

Taking Sides

Descartes claimed that we have inner awareness of how our minds cause motion in our bodies. In the middle of the 20th century, British philosopher **Gilbert Ryle** called this an illusion, describing it as "the dogma of the ghost in the machine." Mental states are just dispositions to act in certain ways.

For instance, the belief that it is raining is not some private event in my head, but my disposition is to bring an umbrella or to say yes when you ask if it is raining.

Ryle uses an analogy: Suppose you visit a university and see all the campus buildings. When the tour is over, you ask, "But where is the university?" You have made what Ryle calls a category mistake. The university is not a building, but a way of talking about all the buildings, plus some policies, a history, and other things. Similarly, the mind is not a thing existing alongside the body, but a way of talking *about* the body.

Consider This

- How are thinking and consciousness different? Could there be a thinking machine that is not conscious?

- Do you think animals like bats have consciousness? What about insects?

- Does the idea that the mind is just something in the brain sound reasonable to you? Why or why not?

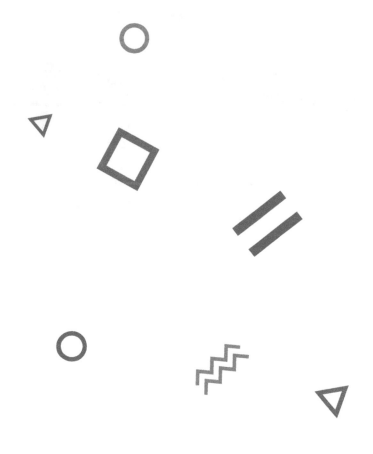

CHAPTER 3

Epistemology: What Can We Know?

pistemology is the study of what we know and how we know it. Importantly, it's also the study of what we don't and can't know.

Different claims typically require different sorts of evidence. If you're wondering what the weather will be, who committed a crime, or where you left your book, there are different procedures for figuring out the answer to each of those questions. Philosophers look closely at those kinds of procedures, and also invent new ones intended to justify—or rule out—knowledge about philosophical topics.

HOW DO WE KNOW THINGS?

We assume that we know many things, but how does this work? Are some ways of getting knowledge better than others? Are some of them foundational, so that the rest of our knowledge builds on them?

Philosophers want to better understand how we evaluate what we see and hear and figure out if our current ways of knowing can be improved. If we have too much confidence in our ability to know things, we could end up with a lot of false beliefs. At the same time, we don't want to miss out on believing important truths because we don't trust ourselves.

WHO ASKED IT?

In around the 2nd century BCE, **Akshapada Gautama**'s Nyaya-sutras tried to list all the different ways we know things:

- **Perception:** Learning through our senses

- **Inference:** Using reasoning, like when you see an effect (smoke) and thereby know its cause (fire)

- **Comparison:** When you already know one object ("I know a dog is an animal") and so can conclude something about a similar one ("I can know a wolf is an animal, too, since it's like a dog")

- **Testimony:** Believing a trustworthy person

Nyaya philosophers thought this list covered all the different possible cases of knowledge.

WHO ANSWERED IT?

Around 400 years later, the Nyaya commentator **Vatsyayana** considered possible objections to the Nyaya-sutras' list. For one, he said of atoms, when I see a tree, I see it as one thing, when really it's a lot of little things, so perception must be wrong. Vatsyayana argued that the whole tree is a thing, too, just as real as the atoms that are part of it, and we know this because perception clearly tells us so.

Plato claimed that knowledge is a puzzle: You can only try to gain knowledge if you already know what you're looking for. For instance, I can only recognize something as a tree if I already know what a tree is. Plato argued that we must be born already knowing everything we could possibly know, and learning is just remembering. In other words, we become conscious of what we unconsciously already know.

The 17th-century English philosopher **John Locke** thought this idea of being born with knowledge was nonsense. People, he said, are like an empty chalkboard, waiting for their senses to fill them up with knowledge.

Locke thought we can also have *probable* knowledge about things like tiny, imperceptible particles by using analogies. This is similar to what Akshapada Gautama called comparison. For example, I see that rapidly rubbing certain things together causes fire, so I can guess that heat itself is created by little particles rapidly bumping into each other.

Locke's position that all knowledge ultimately has to come from our five senses is called **empiricism**. To him, sense experience must serve as the foundation for all other knowledge.

In Real Life

Empiricism sounds very sensible—seeing is believing, right? But we rely on testimony, or people telling us things, for a lot of our beliefs. If you've never been to Australia, then you're relying on others' testimony that it really exists. Even if you got on a plane and went there, you'd be relying on the testimony of the airline, the people you met there, and posted signs to tell you that you were in Australia. They could all be lying. It could be just a big prank on you, and you're really still in your hometown. What have we experienced directly that justifies belief in testimony?

Taking Sides

The opposite of empiricism is rationalism, which is the idea that reason—not sense experience—provides us with the most basic and important knowledge.

An empiricist claims that among the four ways to know things on Akshapada Gautama's list, perception is basic. We can use reason to make inferences or decide to believe testimony, but, they would argue, reason by itself tells us nothing.

For a rationalist like Plato, perception doesn't work without reason. When you perceive something, you use concepts. You see a dog using concepts you're already familiar with: dog, animal, alive, furry.

It seems like we learn concepts from our parents telling us what words mean, which involves testimony and our senses. But what gives us the ability to understand and communicate these concepts? Plato thought that concepts really come from reason, not the senses.

Consider This

- Try to explain why we should believe this sentence: "Most people tell the truth most of the time."

- Have you ever actually seen a triangle? Keep in mind that according to geometry, the lines of a triangle are perfectly straight and have no width, and the whole triangle has no thickness.

HOW CAN WE BE SURE ABOUT ANYTHING?

There are lots of facts we think we know, but could we be wrong about most or even all of them? Maybe people are actually lying to us. Or maybe life is just a long dream, and I'm the only real person who exists. Or maybe I'm not really a person at all.

How can we be sure that our senses are telling us the truth? Or that when we reason, or use what people call common sense, we aren't making a mistake? If we're wrong about our real situation in the world, we could be doing all the wrong things.

WHO ASKED IT?

Around 300 BCE, the Greek philosopher **Pyrrho**—who, like Socrates, never wrote any books—inspired a tradition of **skepticism** about the senses. We know that our senses mislead us sometimes. The sun looks pretty small in the sky, but it is actually enormous. If you take a straight stick and place it in a glass of water, it will look bent. If your hand is very cold and you put it in room-temperature water, the water feels hot, but if your hand is already hot, that same water will feel cool.

If our senses sometimes lie, why should we ever trust them?

WHO ANSWERED IT?

Skepticism is a philosophy that tends to be a response to earlier philosophers who claimed to have all the answers. In India, Vedic philosophers thought they had figured out what the world was like, and then the Buddhists (among others) came along and skeptically questioned them. Pyrrho reportedly spent a year and a half in India and may have gotten his ideas there.

Nagarjuna, who was Buddhist, used skepticism to question beliefs that he thought led to suffering. Importantly, Buddhists question whether we each really have a **self** that persists over time. We all have experiences, but we don't actually perceive an underlying self or soul that has all those experiences. If we have no reason to believe in a self, then a lot of the things that typically worry us are based on a mistake.

Likewise, the goal of Pyrrho's skepticism was tranquility. He argued that if we can't know much of anything, then we can stop worrying about philosophical questions.

René Descartes used skeptical questioning to try to figure out what we really know for sure. Unlike the Buddhists, he thought that the self is the only thing we're certain about. His famous saying "I think, therefore I am" means that even if you're dreaming and everything your senses are telling you is a lie, there must be some self that is having the dream and being lied to. Descartes thought that our certainty about ourselves is enough to provide a foundation for the rest of what we know.

In Real Life

Scientists should be skeptical about what they think they know. This keeps them asking questions, which helps science advance over time.

But believing that our senses can *never* be trusted would make science impossible. Not only that, we couldn't get along in the world. If you're about to be hit by a bus, stopping to ponder whether the bus might be an illusion is unwise. (Though one story tells us that Pyrrho never looked where he was going, so his friends had to save him from being hit by carts; he was more likely only skeptical about philosophical theories.)

Taking Sides

Descartes thought that the existence of yourself is self-evident, which means that something is just obvious to anyone who thinks about it. You don't have to look for evidence that it's true that you exist; just the fact that you're thinking at all makes it true beyond any skeptical doubts.

The empiricist David Hume disagreed. Like the Buddhists, he was skeptical about the existence of a self over time. He argued that what we actually experience is a series of thoughts and perceptions. We don't actually perceive a self that connects all these together.

Descartes thought that we have to start with self-evident truths given to us by reason, and use those to judge less reliable sources of information like our senses. But if Hume was right about the self, then Descartes was wrong about the one thing he thought he was most certain about, and so he thoroughly lost his fight against skepticism.

Consider This

- Do you agree with the skeptics that philosophical questions just cause us to worry, and we're better off just shrugging and saying that we can't really know anything?

- Assume that the skeptic is right and we can't really be *certain* about anything. Who cares? Do we even need certainty?

ARE THERE SOME THINGS WE JUST CAN'T KNOW?

A definition for "knowledge" common by the 17th century but perhaps traceable back to Plato is "justified true belief." It makes sense that we can only know something that's true and that we can only know something if we believe it, but what about the "justified" part?

Scientists theorize about what happened millions of years before we were born or what's going on in parts of the universe we've never seen. Metaphysicians talk about the causes of our experience and the existence of God. Can these speculations possibly be justified, or are there some areas that will remain forever unknown to us?

WHO ASKED IT?

In the 12th century, the Spanish Jewish philosopher **Moses Maimonides** thought very hard about what human reason is capable of. He argued that while we can learn physics, astronomy—the study of space and the physical universe—is beyond us.

Maimonides was most famous for his **negative theology**: What God is like is beyond human comprehension, but we can say plenty about what God is *not* like. We can't know that God is all-powerful and all-knowing, but we can know that God exists and is *not* limited in power and knowledge and other abilities the way humans are.

WHO ANSWERED IT?

Empiricists like David Hume drew a hard line between things we can know and things we can't: We can do scientific experiments that rely on human experience, and we can also do mathematics, but any philosophy that goes beyond those is just garbage.

However, Hume's empiricist contemporary **George Berkeley** disagreed, saying that we actually *know* that everything we see is only made up of ideas in our minds and in God's mind. This view is called **idealism**. Berkeley thought that the idea of mind-independent matter just didn't make any sense.

Immanuel Kant responded by drawing a distinction between the part of the world that we experience and can investigate, which he called the **phenomenal world**, and the world as it really is, which he called the **noumenal world**: a world beyond our knowledge. For example, we can't argue about whether God exists or how the universe began, or whether materialism (that everything you see is really matter) or idealism (that everything you see is only an idea) is true. Note that even though we can't *know* the noumenal world, we can have *faith* about it.

Kant thought that we can know a lot about the phenomenal world, because it's actually our minds that create what we experience. Our minds project space, time, causality, substance, and other categories of existence onto phenomena. We can be absolutely certain, for instance, that every effect has a cause, because our minds are what put causality into the world we experience.

In Real Life

You can bite into an apple to assure yourself that it's really an apple. You can weigh it, measure it, or put it under a microscope, and as long as your tools to do these things are working properly, then it looks like you've gained some knowledge.

However, you can't decide by doing this whether a materialist like Epicurus is right that the apple is just made up of matter (like atoms) or whether an idealist like Berkeley is right that the apple is really just an idea. Since there's no practical difference between these two positions, some philosophers have argued that the distinction is meaningless.

Taking Sides

All empiricists agree that we know the world only through the senses. We all experience apples, so apples most likely exist, but what do we actually sense? We sense qualities like "red," "round," "juicy," and "sweet."

David Hume thought that this is *all* an apple is: just a bundle of qualities. John Locke thought that there must also be something that has those qualities, even though we don't experience it directly: a substance.

Locke thought that substances are mind-independent, which means they exist whether or not anyone is thinking of them. George Berkeley thought that this concept of a mind-independent substance is self-contradicting; apples must just be ideas in minds. Berkeley argued that everything we can think of has the quality of being thought of, which means it's not mind-independent.

Try to think of an apple that no one is thinking of. You can't, because you're thinking of it right now!

Consider This

- If you put a book down and leave the room, you assume that the book is still there unless someone else moved it. Why?

- Are you convinced by Berkeley's argument that there can be no mind-independent reality? Why or why not?

- Do you think we can have knowledge without it being justified?

WHAT IS TRUTH?

Typically when we say or think or believe something, we try to be truthful. We want our words and mind to represent the world accurately.

We might be mistaken or lying in specific instances, but if people weren't normally telling the truth, we wouldn't even be able to make sense of language. Imagine if your teachers lied to you constantly while teaching you what words mean!

So we must all already understand what truth is. But one thing philosophy teaches us is that it's often hard to articulate what we know, and we might find out that we're wrong.

WHO ASKED IT?

The 13th-century Italian Catholic philosopher **Thomas Aquinas** characterized the traditional theory of truth by saying that a judgment is true when it conforms to external reality. This is called the correspondence theory of truth: a belief or statement matches the way the world is.

Aquinas thought that we can know many important philosophic truths, but his definition actually traces back to a 2nd-century BCE Greek skeptic named **Carneades** as a way of *doubting* our ability to know truth. If truth involves comparing our beliefs to the world, how could we access the world directly to check whether it matches a belief?

WHO ANSWERED IT?

If truth is a matter of something in the mind matching something in a mind-independent world, that spells trouble for philosophers like Berkeley, who didn't believe there is a mind-independent world, and Kant, who thought that we can't know anything about a mind-independent world.

Instead of comparing beliefs to the world, an alternative is to compare them to other beliefs. Do your beliefs fit together without contradicting each other? This is called a **coherence theory of truth**. According to this idea, a new belief you're considering will be defined as true if it fits with the rest of your beliefs.

Philosophers holding a coherence theory of truth included Baruch Spinoza—who thought that an object and the idea we have of it are literally one and the same thing, just seen from different points of view—and the early-20th-century British idealist **Harold Joachim**, who argued that a belief is true if it fits in with a systematic, consistent worldview.

In the late 1800s, American philosopher **Charles Sanders Peirce** came up with the **pragmatic theory of truth**: Truth is whatever opinion would eventually be agreed upon by researchers who worked on a problem long enough. Is Earth flat or round? Historical researchers performing tests eventually agreed that it's round.

The American pragmatist **William James** defined truth as what *works*, what we can act on. Is it true that there's a snake in my boot? If that belief lets me avoid being bitten, then yes!

In Real Life

According to William James, a belief is not something that is in itself true or false, but it is *made true* by things that happen. For example, let's say you believe that you don't have any math homework due tomorrow. The next day, your teacher asks you to turn in your homework. That belief didn't work out so well for you, right? So it was false.

But if there ends up being an emergency assembly during math class, or if the teacher forgets to collect the homework, then James would argue that your belief has turned out to be true!

Taking Sides

Coherence and pragmatic theories of truth are attractive because they start with how people actually make decisions about what is true. If I believe that it's raining, I can confirm if this is true by going outside to check.

This is also what I'd do according to the correspondence theory, but checking outside might not be enough. Maybe what I think I'm sensing isn't actually rain. Maybe it's an illusion, or I'm having a dream. My belief might still not match the facts of the real world.

The coherence and pragmatic theories argue that our beliefs should be considered true unless some conflict arises with one of them, like if my belief that it is raining is contradicted by the fact that I'm now experiencing dry weather.

The correspondence theory says this is cheating. Reality just is what it is, regardless of any beliefs anyone might have about it.

Consider This

- Do you think we even need a theory of truth? Or is truth just something so basic that it can't even be defined?

- If there's some fact no one could ever possibly know, could it still be a fact?

- Is it possible that all your beliefs could be false?

HOW IS SCIENCE DIFFERENT FROM OTHER KINDS OF KNOWING?

The philosophy of science is a branch of philosophy that has grown off epistemology. Instead of just wondering how we know things in everyday circumstances, or how we can know abstract metaphysical truths, we're interested here in how scientists do what they do. What is the scientific method? What counts as scientific evidence? How does science progress over time?

People have always investigated the natural world, and ancient philosophers like Aristotle, Thales, the physician **Galen**, and the astronomer **Ptolemy** documented their observations of the world. But modern science with its distinct methods of investigation didn't come into practice until around the 16th century.

WHO ASKED IT?

The British thinker **Francis Bacon** has been regarded as the inventor of the scientific method, which involves systematic experimentation in an attempt to impartially gather facts. He asked what was preventing the growth of knowledge and identified biases that he thought were getting in the way.

Some of these biases are built into human nature: We tend to exaggerate and make up stories about things we really know nothing about. Some biases result from education. For example, if you study chemistry, you tend to think there must be a chemical solution to every problem. We're also fooled by the uses of words, which may not actually reflect the realities they supposedly represent. For example, we say the sun rises, when really it's Earth that's rotating while the sun remains stationary.

Bacon thought that we need to abandon the false knowledge given by past speculation and philosophy, and instead use experiments to collect facts about the world in a foolproof way that everyone can agree on. He thought that science seeks facts about cause and effect, and that we can be absolutely certain about the facts scientists identify using his method. With this method, our knowledge will just grow and grow over time.

WHO ANSWERED IT?

In the 1930s, the Austrian British philosopher **Karl Raimund Popper** claimed that an experiment can't prove a scientific theory. For example, if I'm trying to prove that gravity makes all heavy objects fall, I can't demonstrate this no matter how many objects I drop.

Astronauts have now shown that objects are weightless in outer space. They don't fall at all; they just float. This observation shows that my proposed theory of gravity was false. Popper thought that science progresses not through confirmations (showing that a theory is true) but refutations (showing that a theory is false). Scientific method involves devising experiments to try to **refute** a theory. If these experiments fail to show that the theory is false, then we can keep accepting it, *for now.*

In 1962, the American historian of science **Thomas Kuhn** argued that scientific worldviews—which he called **paradigms**—aren't refuted by experiments. When an experiment seems to show a paradigm is wrong, instead of giving up the paradigm, the scientist typically concludes that something was wrong with the experiment or just dismisses the result as something we can't explain yet. Kuhn thought that changes in paradigm are like changes in fashion and occur mostly because young scientists replace older ones.

In the 1980s, the Hungarian philosopher **Imré Lakatos** described science as people pursuing different "research programs" (his replacement for the concept of a paradigm), which are made up of core theories surrounded by less important claims.

All theories are born refuted, Lakatos said. For instance, when **Isaac Newton**'s laws of motion became widely accepted, scientists already knew that they didn't explain the weird way the planet Mercury moves in the sky, in an unusually noncircular orbit. This is the kind of observation Popper would have claimed refutes the theory. But instead of abandoning the laws of motion, Newtonian scientists claimed that there must be some other planet closer to the sun that interferes with Mercury's orbit. (There isn't.)

It wasn't until the 20th century that **Albert Einstein** invented a different research program for physics that explained Mercury's movement and also made other predictions about things no one had previously thought to investigate, like that the measurable distance between stars is different during the day than at night. Making new, startling discoveries is for Lakatos what makes one research program better than another, but that doesn't mean the less predictive program has been refuted.

In Real Life

According to Kuhn and Lakatos, when we learn something that contradicts our beliefs, we try to change them as little as possible.

For instance, let's assume you think your teacher is smart and well educated, and wants to help you. If you find out that something this teacher told you was incorrect, the easiest way to understand what has happened is that a simple mistake was made.

You'd have to see lots more cases of bad information from that teacher before you'd change your more central beliefs and conclude that actually, the teacher is poorly informed, not smart, or lying to you.

Taking Sides

Bacon and Popper agreed that scientific progress was rational and inevitable, so long as the scientific method was being used correctly.

Kuhn denied this. Inside a given paradigm, Kuhn thought that scientists can make reliable progress as they gather more information. However, each paradigm makes core assumptions that are never questioned, and this puts a limit on scientific progress.

For example, most natural scientists will not accept a scientific conclusion that relies on supernatural elements like mind reading or ghosts. Likewise, Newtonian physicists would not seriously consider the idea that space is curved, which is what Einstein eventually concluded. Kuhn didn't think that later paradigms were necessarily better than earlier ones.

Lakatos argued that even though scientific progress is not a simple matter of rationally paying attention to experimental results, we can distinguish what he called progressive research programs—which make unforeseen discoveries—from research programs that are in decline.

- Do you think science always moves forward toward truth, or could it actually be getting more things wrong over time? Why?

- Do you feel there are some questions you're too biased to answer impartially? Why or why not?

- Think about an experiment you might perform and two opposing ways to interpret its results.

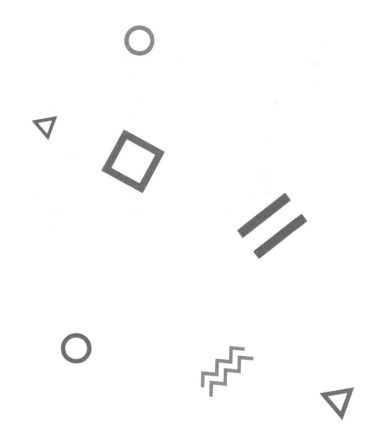

CHAPTER 4

Ethics: What Are We Supposed to Do?

Ethics is about right and wrong. The word **"morality"** often refers to your personal code of conduct, while "ethics" is about a professional code (like medical ethics). Don't worry about this difference. You can just use either word.

Everyone has opinions about good and bad behavior. Are some of those opinions correct and others incorrect? Which ones?

DOES BEING GOOD MEAN DIFFERENT THINGS TO DIFFERENT PEOPLE?

Some people like chocolate ice cream. Some prefer vanilla, or chocolate chip cookie dough. Some don't like ice cream at all. None of these groups is wrong. Is morality just like that?

If so, then morality is subjective, or a matter of individual taste. Just an opinion, with nothing more to be said about it. No philosophy needed!

It's interesting, though, that there's so much agreement about morality, especially among members of the same society. A society's customs—what is considered normal according to that society's traditions—include many opinions about correct behavior: what to eat, how to express respect, etc.

WHO ASKED IT?

A few decades before Socrates died, the Greek historian **Herodotus** wondered about the wildly different moral beliefs among various foreign lands. For instance, the Greeks buried their dead out of respect, while some other cultures would eat their dead, also out of respect. Each group thought their customs were morally correct.

Herodotus wondered, if ethics were the kind of thing we could investigate, if there were objective facts about morality that we could all look for, then why haven't people all over the world reached the same moral conclusions? Maybe what you consider right is just a result of where you were born.

WHO ANSWERED IT?

Around 500 BCE, the Chinese politician and philosopher **Confucius** (also known as Kongzi) claimed that his ethic was to live in harmony with nature. This doesn't mean living out in the wilderness. Confucius thought that society is part of nature, so being in tune with nature means doing our duty as society has defined it. This will, of course, be different for different societies.

Aristotle thought that ethics is something we can investigate scientifically, because it's part of human nature. We can study what's good for any animal by watching it grow. Humans, like other animals, try to grow healthy and strong, so that's part of our good. But unlike other animals, we can also think, and Aristotle claimed that thinking well is our highest good as humans.

In the early 19th century, English philosopher and jurist **Jeremy Bentham** argued that ethics can be investigated scientifically in a different way: by paying attention to what brings us pleasure and pain. He defined a right action as one that produces the most pleasure and the least pain for the most people.

The early-20th-century American anthropologist **Ruth Benedict** used her scientific study of different cultures to argue that morality is entirely relative to culture, and that we should respect other cultures' moral standards. When we encounter values and customs that seem strange to us, we can try to understand why they make sense to those people by studying their culture.

In Real Life

Every society has its own customs and makes ethical judgments from its own point of view. We can ask whether something is wrong according to the customs of this country or that country, but thinkers like Benedict claim there's no way to decide which norms are better.

For example, in some countries, women are not allowed to be outside without a male relative, while in other countries, women are able to move as freely as they'd like. In some countries, drinking alcohol and gambling are permitted, while in others, these activities are considered immoral. Do you agree with Benedict?

Taking Sides

Confucius was a political advisor and wanted society to be well ordered and peaceful. Everyone should work to become more respectful, dutiful, and humane. We should try to measure up to the standards that have been handed down through our society's traditions. This will put us in harmony with the natural order of the universe.

Another long intellectual tradition in China is Daoism, whose founder, **Laozi** (also known as Lao-tzu), lived around the time of Confucius. The Chinese word *dao* means "way" or "path": how people ought to behave. Laozi also taught living in harmony with nature, but thought that this has nothing to do with society. The Dao is the force that flows through everything, holding us together and giving us direction. Society's expectations and norms are just a distraction from the Dao. All of us should withdraw and think deeply, and we'll naturally become peaceful, kind, and selfless.

Consider This

- Do you think that scientists can study what is actually right and wrong, or only what various cultures have said is right and wrong?

- What are some customs in your own culture that you think are right or wrong? Pick one that you think is wrong; why do you think that?

WHAT KIND OF PERSON SHOULD I BE?

We often think about ethics as a matter of rules. If you follow the right rules, you're doing the right thing.

But rules and actions are not always the way we think about ethics. If you ask, What would so-and-so do? you're

not asking about a set of rules. You've identified someone (real or not) you want to be like. And you pick people to emulate because they have **virtues** you'd like to have. You want to be heroic or saintly or a genius. If you had those virtues, you'd always know what to do.

WHO ASKED IT?

Plato, Aristotle, Confucius, and Laozi all taught virtue ethics. For these thinkers, human nature comes with built-in goals. Achieving these goals makes you successfully human: virtuous.

For Aristotle, fulfilling our human potential doesn't require becoming a superhuman saint or sage. The key to virtue is *moderation*. Eat too little and you'll starve, but eat too much and you'll be unhealthy. The virtue of moderation here is called temperance.

The same goes for virtues like bravery: Not enough bravery is cowardice. Too much is foolishness. The central virtue is wisdom, which enables us to find the virtuous middle path.

WHO ANSWERED IT?

Thomas Aquinas's overall project was to combine Aristotle's thinking with Christianity. Aquinas thought virtue and rules are inseparable. To be virtuous is to have a conscience that gives you moral principles. "Love thy neighbor" is the supreme principle.

The 18th-century German philosopher **Friedrich Nietzsche** also thought we should pay attention to our nature to figure out how to become the best version of ourselves but denied that we all have exactly the same human nature. We all want to thrive, but another person's thriving might not look like your thriving. There is no single ethical ideal we should imitate. Instead, we each need to create our own unique way of being great.

Current Scottish American philosopher **Alasdair MacIntyre** modernized Aristotle's idea of built-in goals by looking at the goals built into activities we already engage in, like cooking or guitar playing. When we try to do them, we try to do them *well*, according to standards we've inherited from our culture. The overall human goal is to fit together all those ways we're trying to do well—to *integrate* those smaller goals—into one coherent life: a life with **integrity**.

The 20th-century British novelist and philosopher **Iris Murdoch** argued that virtue is a matter of being sensitive to what each situation morally requires of us. Look outward, not just inward. She said, "In the moral life, the enemy is the fat, relentless **ego**." To be virtuous, get over yourself and pay attention!

In Real Life

If you think about what an ideally moral person would be like, you might think of someone who is always very careful to put other people first and obey moral rules.

Aristotle thought the best way to behave ethically is to develop your character so you can make calm, reasoned decisions. This actually requires paying a lot of attention to yourself. You should eat healthily, get lots of exercise and enough sleep, and, most important, surround yourself with admirable people from whom you can learn. Only through self-care will you be strong enough to behave ethically.

Taking Sides

Alasdair MacIntyre was following Aristotle (and Nietzsche) in trying to ground moral action in types of excellence that we don't normally think of as part of morality. Being talented, smart, perceptive, and persuasive are impressive and useful traits. Surely people with those traits can best figure out what to do, right?

Immanuel Kant denied this, insisting that the only thing that makes an action good is a good will, which means wanting to do the morally right thing. If someone with bad intentions is smart, talented, and perceptive, that only makes them worse. An impressive criminal does more harm than a stupid one.

The question here is how moral values relate to other values we might have. Aristotle thought that figuring out what makes people happy is the first step in studying ethics, but Kant insisted that being ethical means doing your duty, whether or not that makes you happy.

Consider This

- Do you think it matters what kind of person you are, or only that you do the right things?

- Do you agree with Nietzsche that everybody's ideal should be different? Should morality apply differently to different people?

- Do you think selflessness is essential to virtue? Why or why not?

CAN PEOPLE BE GOOD WITHOUT RELIGION?

Have you ever heard someone say, "If you don't believe in God, you have no moral compass"? Maybe you've even said something like that yourself. If morality can be given only by the Bible, the Torah, the Quran, or any other religious scripture, then people with different beliefs will never agree on morality.

Nonetheless, most people agree about important moral principles, including the principles that killing is wrong, hurting is bad, and compassion is good. Why is that? Is it just because of the influence of religion on society, so that even nonbelievers have moral beliefs that came from religion?

WHO ASKED IT?

Plato was a very religious person, and his dialogue *Euthyphro* asks: "Do the gods love pious acts because they are pious, or are those acts pious because the gods love them?"

Plato's answer is that some things are just objectively good (like being pious), and the gods know that. They want us to do those things.

It is *not* the case that the gods could just choose any old thing and *declare* it good. If a book says that God has issued a decree that murder is great, the book must be lying, or you've misunderstood what you've read.

WHO ANSWERED IT?

Plato's answer means that a good religious commandment will have a reason behind it; it will make sense. This means it might be possible for any of us—religious or not—to figure out ethics. Plato thought we're all naturally drawn to the good, that it's inside us like a forgotten memory. Philosophy is all about trying to bring it to the surface.

Augustine of Hippo was an Algerian philosopher and bishop in 400 CE who instead adopted the divine command theory. The theory says, no, it's only God's commands that make good things good. Augustine thought that since everyone is born sinful, we can't figure out ethics on our own, and even when we know what's right, we often sin.

Immanuel Kant agreed with Plato that people are able to know fundamental moral truths without looking to any religious text. Kant thought these truths were given by reason itself. Even aliens from another world, as long as they were rational, thinking beings, could figure out ethics.

The 19th-century Danish philosopher **Søren Kierkegaard** agreed with Kant's ethical theory, but argued that religion overrules ethics: We should put trust in God, even if God's commands seem unethical to us.

The 20th-century British Catholic philosopher **Elizabeth Anscombe** argued that our language for talking about morality was developed with a law-giving God in mind. Talking about moral rules and obligations only makes sense if there's a rule-maker we're obliged to obey. Giving up religion means having to rethink ethics entirely.

In Real Life

Hermeneutics is the study of how we do and should interpret texts. Religious figures as far back as **Origen of Alexandria** in the 2nd century CE and Augustine in the 4th claimed that parts of the Bible are metaphorical, and it was only during the 18th century that biblical literalism—the idea that the Bible is clear enough for the average person to understand without possibility of error—became prominent.

Questions to ask when interpreting an ethical commandment in a religious text include: What was the social context in which this command was issued? Who was it directed to? What other commands are made in that part of the text?

Taking Sides

Augustine was highly influenced by Plato. Both of them saw reason as a requirement for being virtuous. Reason has to be put in charge of your soul. It has to control your desires and emotions.

For Plato, when reason is in charge, we become more spiritual. It's like we're emerging from a dark cave and can finally see the light of eternal goodness. We become more godlike, and we'll know the right things to do. Reading a book can help *remind* us of our holy nature, but that nature is always in us.

Augustine saw people as essentially sinful. He believed that people are cut off from goodness and truth, but can know God's commands through scriptures and faith. Putting reason in charge frees us up to do what God wants, and it helps us interpret scripture, but faith is the primary virtue.

Consider This

- Do you think having religious beliefs makes people more ethical? Why or why not?

- What do you think of this quote from Russian novelist **Fyodor Dostoyevsky**: "If there is no God, everything is permitted"?

- Do you think that reason tells us what is right and wrong? Why or why not?

ARE PEOPLE RESPONSIBLE FOR THEIR ACTIONS?

Many philosophers—**and** even more scientists—see nature as one big machine. Everything has a cause, including human behavior. People act the way they do because of how their brains work, how their parents treated them, how they were educated, and all sorts of other circumstances.

How can this allow for moral choices? If I only choose what I do because of forces beyond my control, should I be blamed or praised for any of my actions?

The idea that people's actions are controlled by natural causes, not by their free choices, is called **determinism**.

WHO ASKED IT?

The 1st-century CE Greek **Epictetus** was an important philosopher in the Stoic tradition, which emphasized realizing what is and is not in our power. Stoics preach that we can't control our circumstances, but we can control how we react to them.

Epictetus thought that the universe is controlled by destiny, but you can still be free by separating yourself from the demands of your body, including your emotions and desires. You are only your will, your ability to make decisions and take action, and you shouldn't let other parts of your mind distract you from your duty or make you unhappy.

WHO ANSWERED IT?

In around 500 CE, the Roman senator **Boethius** rephrased the question in religious terms: How can we choose freely when God knows everything we will choose beforehand? If God sees our future choices, that means that they are, in a sense, already fixed, so freedom seems like it must be an illusion. Boethius's response was that God can somehow allow us to be free despite God's omniscience.

Thomas Hobbes was a determinist; people's actions are determined by their character, which is a result of their nature and education. No one is really responsible for their actions, but we can still distinguish between actions that are forced by an external cause—like if someone has a gun to your head—and actions that are your own.

Immanuel Kant argued that in order to make moral decisions, we have to act as if we are free, even though science tells us we are determined. Even though people *seem* determined, we can't know our true nature, and this ignorance leaves us room to have faith in our own freedom.

William James also thought we can simply choose to believe our choices are free. This assumption works well to help us run our lives. Believing that we have free will causes us to make better decisions.

The 20th-century British philosopher **Peter Frederick Strawson** argued that praise and blame are central to the way we deal with each other. We couldn't give them up even if we tried. It doesn't matter if determinism is true; we must still regard people as morally responsible.

In Real Life

If someone hurts you, you probably want to know why. Was it an accident? If it was intentional, that means the person meant to hurt you. If the person was impaired somehow (drunk, sick, etc.), you might judge their actions differently.

Punishing a criminal, for a determinist, is like punishing a dog that has bitten someone. We might lock up the dog to keep people safe, or even euthanize it, but this isn't punishment. We don't consider a dog capable of making moral choices. What would it be like to always treat people this way?

Taking Sides

P. F. Strawson's son **Galen Strawson**, also a philosopher, disagreed with his father's position that long-standing, unchangeable social practices force us to regard each other as morally responsible.

Instead, Galen argued that no one can be held morally responsible. Why not? Because people make choices based on their character—their personality—but no one chooses their personality. Of course, we make choices that might help develop our personality, such as choosing between just watching TV all day or reading a book that might help me become a better person. But which choice I make will also be a result of my character. Therefore, free will is an illusion.

Both Strawsons believed their position to be true regardless of whether we're all determined by the causal patterns that make up the natural world. That metaphysical issue is not relevant to how we decide to treat each other.

Consider This

- Think of an important choice you made recently. Do you think you could have made a different choice? Why or why not?

- If you think people aren't really responsible for their actions, you can be more forgiving to people who hurt you. Do you think such forgiveness is a good idea? Why or why not?

WHAT'S THE BASIC RULE OF MORALITY?

We've already asked whether there are any real moral rules at all. If morality is a matter of taste, or custom, then there can't be moral rules that apply to everyone. If morality is whatever wise people would choose to do, or whatever the gods happen to command, then you don't need to understand the rules. Just take their word for it!

But philosophy is about questioning. We want to understand *why* those rules are best. We're looking for the reason behind them, a first moral principle.

WHO ASKED IT?

One of the oldest civilizations we know about is Babylonia, which was part of Mesopotamia and encompassed the area from the Persian Gulf to around where Baghdad is today. The Code of Hammurabi is a Babylonian legal text from about 1750 BCE, established by the king of Babylonia, **Hammurabi**.

This code is famous for giving us one of the first moral principles: "An eye for an eye." This is *lex talionis*, a "law of retribution in kind": If someone does something bad—like pokes out someone's eye—then that thing should be done back to them.

This is an early version of the golden rule: Treat others as you would like to be treated. Some version of this rule can be found in virtually every widespread religion.

Another ancient text asking for a basic moral rule is the Bhagavad Gita, a scripture written in India at some point between 400 BCE and 200 CE by the legendary sage **Vyasa**.

The Gita depicts a dialogue: Right before a battle, the warrior prince Arjuna argues that war is obviously bad. It harms everyone involved. His divine chariot driver Krishna replies that Arjuna's duty (his dharma) overrules this. Arjuna is a warrior, and this is a just war, so it's his duty to play his part in it, despite his concerns. The fundamental moral rule is to always selflessly do your duty.

WHO ANSWERED IT?

Jeremy Bentham's position that the right act produces the most pleasure and least pain for the most people is called **utilitarianism**. The 19th-century English utilitarian **John Stuart Mill** revised Bentham's theory to say that the right act will maximize happiness, not pleasure. Mill thought that overall happiness was a better goal than pleasure because not all pleasures make us happy, and that pleasures of the mind matter more for morality than feelings of physical pleasure.

The 20th-century English philosopher **Bernard Williams** argued that utilitarianism doesn't work because it goes against living with integrity. Integrity means your life fits together: You are a person with your own personality, commitments, and projects. Utilitarianism says that when you're figuring out what's right, you have to just ignore all that and in each moment do whatever will bring the most benefit to the most people. Williams thought this would be a crazy way to live.

Immanuel Kant believed that our ability to reason shows us absolute moral rules that should be followed in all circumstances. You should always do your duty, and you can tell what your duty is by performing this test: When you're thinking of doing something, don't think of its results, but about whether that action could be a law for everyone. For example, if you're thinking about telling a lie, ask yourself: Would it be okay if everyone were allowed to lie all the time? Probably not. If they did, we wouldn't need to have speech at all.

Kant thought that another way of stating this very same moral rule is that we should never *use* people. Of course, we benefit from other people all the time—hopefully by reading this book you're benefiting from me right now—but to use someone is to benefit from them without caring about their interests or consent. If you lie to someone, even if you think it's a harmless lie, you're not treating that person as someone who has a right to make their own decisions.

The early-20th-century English philosopher **G. E. Moore** thought that the right action is whichever one will produce the most good, but argued that we can't describe what the good is in non-moral terms like pleasure or happiness. Instead, he saw goodness as something fundamental that we can all know through intuition. No single principle is going to cover all the different things we consider good.

In Real Life

One practical issue to consider in evaluating a moral theory is what it says about how we should treat animals. For Bentham, animals feel pain and pleasure, so their interests count. For Mill, people can feel more profound sorrow and joy than animals can, so our interests definitely count more.

For Kant, it's our ability to reason that makes us worthy of moral respect, so animals don't count in our moral calculations at all. However, Kant thought that being kind to animals is still a good habit that will make us more likely to behave well to humans.

Taking Sides

Kant's theory says to always tell the truth, but Kant's contemporary **Benjamin Constant** objected with the "murderer at the door" example.

Suppose there's a murderer who is hunting someone who's hiding in your house. The murderer rings your doorbell and asks if his victim is there. If you tell the truth (as Kant advises), the murderer will burst in and kill the victim.

This is a terrible outcome, but Kant said we can't make exceptions when it comes to following moral rules. We don't know what the future will be, so it's always better to make sure your own actions follow the rules.

A utilitarian, according to Kant's argument, is ignoring the important distinction between actively doing wrong and merely letting something bad happen. You can't control the murderer's actions, only your own. If you can help the victim in some other way, you should, but two wrongs won't make a right.

Consider This

- Can you think of a case where "treat others how you want to be treated" would direct you to do something wrong?

- What would you do in the "murderer at the door" scenario?

- What do you think is the best reason to be kind to animals?

CHAPTER 5

Logic: What Is an Argument?

When a philosopher—or anyone else—gives you reasons for believing some claim, that's an argument. An argument doesn't have to be a statement based in anger; sometimes an argument is just part of explaining what a philosophical theory means and why anyone would believe it.

In this chapter, we'll look at some ways to succeed or fail in argumentation. You'll learn some terms and techniques that philosophers have used to evaluate arguments and to make their own arguments stronger.

WHAT'S THE STRONGEST KIND OF ARGUMENT?

There are two things an argument needs to be good: true **premises** and a valid argument form. Premises are your starting point, the reasons you're giving for someone to believe your conclusion, which means the claim you're arguing for.

A valid argument form is one where the premises are connected in the right way to the conclusion. The strongest kind of argument is one where if the premises are true, the conclusion logically *has* to be true. The premises logically imply (or entail or necessitate) the conclusion. This is called a **deductive argument.**

WHO ASKED IT?

Aristotle set out to record how we reason and came up with a highly influential way of thinking about reasoning called the **syllogism**. A syllogism is an argument with two premises and a conclusion, where each sentence says something about a thing or category of things.

For example:

1. All dogs are animals.

2. Spot is a dog.

3. Therefore, Spot is an animal.

There are twenty-four different valid forms of syllogism, which Aristotle set out using capital letters to stand for various types of things, like "All A are B" could mean "All animals are brown."

WHO ANSWERED IT?

Over a century later, in the 3rd century BCE, the Greek Stoic philosopher **Chrysippus** created a different way of thinking about logic, which didn't catch on at the time but is now the first type of logic most students learn. This is called sentential logic, because each capital letter stands for a whole sentence. It allows us to clearly see the logical relationships between sentences.

For example, if the letter P means "It is day," and Q means "It is light," then we can say "If it is day, then it is light" by saying "If P, then Q."

These sentences can then be put together in a Stoic syllogism, which captures a simple form of argument called **modus ponens**:

1. If P then Q. [If it is day, then it is light.]

2. P. [It is day.]

3. Therefore, Q. [Therefore it is light.]

In the late 19th century, **Gottlob Frege** developed **predicate logic**. Predicates are descriptions like "is a dog," "is brown," or "is running." We can say "Socrates is running" by saying "Rs."

Frege's biggest innovation is **quantifiers**: "all," symbolized by $\forall$, and "some," symbolized by $\exists$. These quantifiers use variables, which are like names that can refer to anything. So instead of s for Socrates, we can use the variable x.

Here's a predicate logic syllogism with its English translation:

1. $\forall x(Dx \Rightarrow Ax)$ [All dogs are animals.]

2. $\exists x(Dx \ \& \ Hx)$ [Some dogs are hungry.]

3. Therefore, $\exists x(Hx \ \& \ Ax)$ [Some hungry things are animals.]

In Real Life

Don't forget that in addition to a valid argument form, a good argument needs true premises, or at least ones that your opponent in the argument will agree to. Often, one or more of your premises will need its own argument.

If I'm trying to convince you that philosophy is a waste of time, I might argue that it won't get you a high-paying job. The premise that I haven't stated here is that anything that doesn't lead to making a lot of money is a waste of time. If you don't already agree with that idea, then I'd need to argue for it as well.

Taking Sides

An important element of logic is negation, which means saying that some sentences are not true, using the symbol ¬.

In sentential logic, if P means "Dogs are animals" then ¬P (which you'd say out loud as "not P") means "It is not true that dogs are animals."

Why not "Dogs are not animals"? Because in sentential logic, the letter stands for the whole sentence, so that's what you're negating (saying is not true).

In Aristotelian or predicate logic, though, we can also choose to negate just one part of a sentence, changing "All A are B." to "No A are B." or "All A are not B."

"No dogs are animals" and "All dogs are not animals" mean the same thing. But think about ways of negating "All sneezes are blue." It's true that "No sneezes are blue," because sneezes don't have color. But "All sneezes are not blue" implies that they have some other color, which they don't.

Consider This

- Look at the rule modus ponens on page 86. Try to figure out the conclusion of this related rule called modus tollens:

  1. If P, then Q.

  2. Not Q.

  3. Therefore, what?

- What's the difference between negating a sentence—saying that the sentence isn't true—and asserting the opposite of that sentence?

WHAT ARE WAYS AN ARGUMENT CAN GO WRONG?

The point of devising standard argument forms and symbols is to be able to show easily when an argument has the wrong form. For every good argument form, there's at least one wrong version, which is called a formal fallacy. Here's one called affirming the consequent:

1. All dogs are animals.

2. Garfield is an animal.

3. Therefore, Garfield is a dog.

The trickier kinds of fallacies that you really need to watch out for are called informal fallacies, and they can happen as you try to fit your argument into a formal argument form.

WHO ASKED IT?

In ancient Greece, Plato's favorite conversational opponents were Sophists. Sophists were teachers-for-hire, providing lessons in public speaking and argumentation. Like lawyers, they could argue for either side of a case, and Plato didn't like this, because he thought you should only argue what you believe to be true.

Aristotle wrote a book called *Sophistical Refutations* that listed thirteen ways Sophists might twist words around to make deceptive, false arguments. Of course, more often, we just commit these fallacies by mistake. Some of them may represent cases where the people arguing just aren't understanding each other.

WHO ANSWERED IT?

Some of Aristotle's informal fallacies include **equivocation** and **begging the question**.

Equivocation is when a word has two meanings that are treated the same. For example:

1. I have the right to smoke.

2. Therefore, it is right for me to smoke.

Since there are two distinct meanings to "right," the conclusion does not follow.

Begging the question happens when one of your premises relies on the truth of the conclusion. You're assuming the thing you want to argue for. For example: "Everything in this book is true. I know this because the book says so."

The 16th-century theologian **Martin Luther** coined the term "**straw man**" to describe when someone argues against a position his opponent doesn't hold. Luther's opponents claimed that he was against serving Communion, when that was not part of his critique of church practices.

One fallacy discussed by John Locke is the **ad hominem fallacy**. This is when instead of responding to an argument, you just criticize the person making the argument (*ad hominem* is Latin for "to the person"). Doing this means you're not actually engaging the argument at all. A deeply flawed person could still be making a strong argument.

Another fallacy that Locke discussed is appeal to authority, where you claim that because someone says something is true, then it must be true. As a practical matter, we often take the word of experts, but they might be wrong. Especially in philosophy, we can't conclude that a position is correct just because some famous person or text says it is.

Politics is full of straw man and ad hominem arguments. If someone argues that we need strong immigration laws, opponents might simply call that politician racist. Instead of criticizing the idea, the opponents are criticizing the person. Instead, they should argue that the specific immigration laws proposed—which they should characterize accurately—are unnecessarily harsh.

Or a politician might propose that the government provide some new service, and opponents often yell "Socialist!" and complain that the new proposal will make our country into a dictatorship. This is a straw man argument: The opponents are arguing against a position different from the one that's actually being proposed.

Taking Sides

A fallacy that often accompanies straw man and ad hominem argument is the slippery slope, identified by the Roman senator **Cicero** around 50 BCE. This is where someone claims that if we allow some action, steadily worse actions will follow.

For example, should you allow children to swear? Someone could argue that if you let kids swear, then next they'll be talking back to their teachers, then rejecting law altogether! Therefore, children's swearing should be prohibited.

Here the consequences don't logically follow from not swearing, so the argument is fallacious. But some philosophers think that slippery slope arguments don't have to be fallacious. It's just that my example is not very well argued. There's an unstated premise that swearing indicates disrespect. If this is true, then it may actually be true that allowing kids to be disrespectful by swearing will lead to them being disrespectful in other ways.

Consider This

- Some philosophers have claimed that laws of nature are really laws of God. Is this just the fallacy of equivocation using the word "laws"?

- Have you ever dismissed someone else's opinion as described by the ad hominem fallacy?

- Try to think of a slippery slope argument that you think is actually good.

HOW CAN LOGIC HELP WITH SCIENCE?

Early scientists thought that following the scientific method could ensure science never gets anything wrong. But in reality, science can't use deductive arguments. If I observe some particular experimental result, this observation can't serve as a premise in a deductive argument for my scientific theory.

Instead of deduction, science uses **induction**, which is evidence that makes a conclusion more probable. You think the sun will rise tomorrow, right? Why? Because it has always risen in the past. This fact doesn't *ensure* the sun will rise again, but if you've observed many sunrises, it's a reasonable conclusion.

WHO ASKED IT?

Philosophers in ancient India devised logic independently of the Greeks, and their logic was designed as part of epistemology, to help us learn about the world. One of the ways of knowing identified in Akshapada Gautama's Nyaya-sutras is inference, like using the presence of smoke to indicate that there is fire.

Stated as a deductive argument, this would just be modus ponens again:

1. Whenever there is smoke, there is fire.

2. There is smoke.

3. Therefore, there is fire.

However, we also need to justify the first premise, which is an inductive generalization: a theory based on observations of past fires.

WHO ANSWERED IT?

Around 500 CE, the Buddhist logician **Dignaga** analyzed arguments in the form the Nyayas developed, where the conclusion comes first:

1. The hill over there has fire. [The conclusion that we aim to prove]

2. ... because the hill has smoke. [A premise called "the prover"]

3. Whatever has smoke has fire. [The inductive generalization]

4. ... like a fiery kitchen stove. [A supporting example]

There are really two arguments here. Numbers 2 and 3 are premises in a deductive argument for 1. But there's also an inductive argument: The example in 4 provides support for the generalization in 3.

Dignaga described what makes a good prover (smoke, in this case). We want one that fits the example—the stove—but not with any counter-example, which would be something that has smoke without fire, like a smoke machine used at a rock concert.

John Stuart Mill categorized ways to use induction for scientific investigation. For instance, his "method of agreement" says that we should look for a common factor across different instances, and that will be the cause. For instance, if several members of your family—but not all of them—feel nauseous, you might think about whether the sick people (but not the others) all ate the same thing.

David Hume saw induction as an epistemological problem: How can what we've seen justify what we haven't yet seen? We're really just making a guess based on the assumption that nature is consistent, but that assumption is unjustified.

In Real Life

Many of today's inductive arguments use mathematical statistics to support their conclusions. If we want to determine whether a new medicine is safe, or whether most people support a certain political position, we don't have to test or survey every single person, but instead use a representative sample.

Statisticians have developed formulas for the likely amount of error in scientific findings that are based on samples. While it's possible that a drug is safe for *only* those people tested or that randomly chosen survey respondents all have unusual opinions, it's not likely, if the research was conducted properly.

Taking Sides

Around 1950, the German American philosopher Rudolf Carnap tried to develop a system of inductive logic based around Bayes' theorem, a formula for the probability of an event based on some evidence.

For example, if you see smoke and are wondering if it's a dangerous fire and not just someone's barbecue, you'd need to factor in how rare dangerous fires are and how common barbecues are, as well as the high probability that any dangerous fire will emit smoke.

The problem is that Bayes's theorem only tells us probabilities based on other probabilities, so doesn't actually solve the philosophical problem of probability itself, which is essentially the same problem as the one Hume had with induction. How do we know how often dangerous fires will occur? Maybe global warming has changed the world so that these will be much more frequent going forward than they have been in the past.

- "All swans are white" is an inductive generalization. Even if you've seen many white swans, you still might find a black one later. Is "All dogs are animals" also an inductive generalization?

- Can some arguments that look like fallacies actually be reasonable inductive arguments? Can you think of an example?

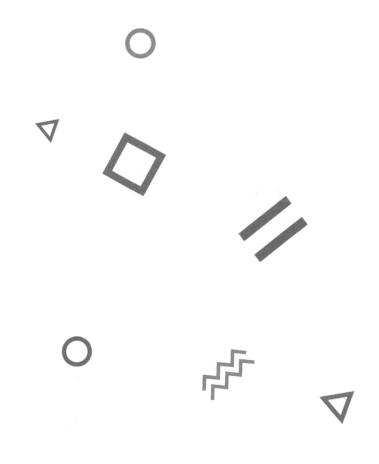

HOW CAN LOGIC HELP WITH ETHICS?

Constructing a good argument requires understanding different kinds of claims. For instance, statements about past and future differ, so "I was reading" doesn't entail that "I will be reading."

In ethics, it's fallacious to conclude that something should be a certain way just because it actually is that way now. For example, "I eat ice cream; therefore, I ought to eat ice cream."

We can understand this difference by distinguishing between facts and values. It is a fact that I eat ice cream, but saying I should do so, or that eating ice cream is good, expresses a value.

WHO ASKED IT?

David Hume challenged past ethics by pointing out this logical difference between facts and values, or what are often called descriptive claims and **normative** claims. The word "normative" says that value claims have something to do with what we think of as normal behavior; norms are standards that a society or culture expects people to live by.

Hume claimed that you can't prove a normative claim using only descriptive premises. For example, utilitarians point to the fact that one action is likely to bring more happiness than another, and think this is reason to perform the action. Hume called this fallacious reasoning.

WHO ANSWERED IT?

Hume claimed that any moral argument must have at least one normative premise, and that premise has to be basic, with no further argument required. If you need to argue for your normative premise, the problem will just repeat. You'd need a more basic normative premise to argue for the first one.

Hume's Scottish contemporary **Adam Smith** pointed to our moral feelings as the basis for morality. We don't need an argument that some things are right and others are wrong, because we already feel this.

Kant likewise argued that his ethical principle was just built into human beings, though he said it came from reason. Utilitarians argued that the principle of utility is self-evident to anyone who really thinks about it. Aristotle thought that human nature already has standards of moral excellence built right in.

The 20th-century French philosopher **Jean-Paul Sartre** took Hume very seriously. Sartre thought we are all radically free, that human nature comes with no guidebook or blueprint, that our good is not determined by any facts of our human nature, and that there is no moral goal that we all find within ourselves. Instead, each of us has the responsibility of deciding our own values.

In Real Life

In life, we typically take fundamental values for granted. If I'm considering whether to steal, I might think about whether doing so would actually hurt anyone or how happy I might be as a thief. I wouldn't think about whether hurting people is bad in general, because that's just assumed.

Hume argues that you couldn't just lay out facts about hurts and happiness and expect to convince someone with no moral feelings or intuitions at all to be moral. If you were trying to program a computer to mimic human moral thinking, you couldn't give it only facts. It would also need commands, like "protect human life."

Taking Sides

Alasdair MacIntyre—whose ethics modernized Aristotle—was not fond of Sartre's existentialism, because he thought it was too whimsical. Existentialism is the opposite of Aristotle's essentialism, which is the idea that humans have an essence that determines what kind of being we are and so what our good is. Our human nature is already fixed before we as individuals are born.

An existentialist switches this formula around to claim that no, it's not essence that comes first, with the existence of the individual coming afterward, but instead we all exist as individuals first, and that our freedom means it's up to us to develop our essence—what kind of creature we want to be.

However, this doesn't mean our choice of values can change according to our whims. Sartre saw this freedom as an intense burden of responsibility and thought we should very carefully consider our actions.

- Construct an argument that stealing is wrong. Are all the premises of your argument descriptive, or is there a normative one there, too?

- If you accept the principle of utility as a premise and argue that a particular action like stealing is wrong, is your argument deductive or inductive?

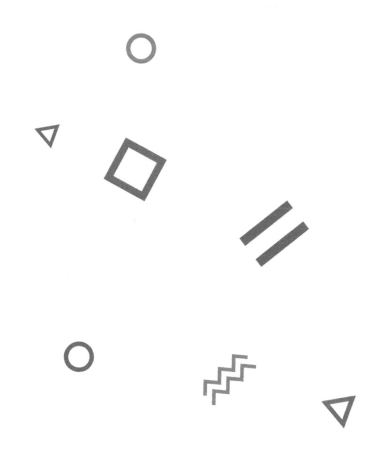

WHAT ELSE CAN PHILOSOPHERS DO WITH LOGIC?

Logic involves analyzing the structure of thought. How do different thoughts relate to each other? Logic is often normative, which means it explores correct ways to think. Some philosophers have even proposed replacing our everyday language—which is filled with vagueness and the danger of fallacies—with a more logically perfect one!

Logic can also be descriptive, as when philosophers just try to understand how different types of philosophical speech work. Usually there's a normative motivation to this, though: We want to look at how we currently think so we decide if this needs improvement.

WHO ASKED IT?

Thinkers like Aristotle and members of the Nyaya school used logic as part of epistemology: to articulate how we reason and make sure we're reasoning well.

Other thinkers used logic as part of an effort to *live* well. For example, Stoics like Chrysippus used it to get rid of irrational thinking that is a barrier to happiness.

This is similar to skeptics like Pyrrho and Buddhists like Nagarjuna who used logic just to refute their opponents, whose views they thought caused needless distress.

Using logic specifically for refutation (arguing against) often uses a technique called **reductio ad absurdum**, which means "reduced to absurdity." Here's how it works: List your opponents' views as premises and show that they result in a contradiction. For example, consider the problem of evil.

1. God exists.

2. God is all-powerful, and so is able to prevent evil.

3. God is good, and so would prevent evil.

4. Evil exists.

5. From 1, 2, and 3, we can deduce that evil does not exist because God has prevented it.

6. From 4, we can conclude that evil exists, and from 5, we can conclude that evil does not exist. This is a contradiction!

A reductio shows that at least one of your opponent's premises must be false.

WHO ANSWERED IT?

In the 20th century, many philosophers built on Gottlob Frege's system of predicate logic to create their own applications to different areas of philosophy:

At the beginning of the century, the English philosophers **Alfred North Whitehead** and **Bertrand Russell** worked to create a foundation for mathematics using symbolic logic. They took over three hundred pages to complete a proof that $1 + 1 = 2$. Ultimately, their project didn't work, not because $1 + 1$ does not equal 2, but because mathematician **Kurt Friedrich Gödel** proved in 1930 that no logical system can include proofs for all the truths of arithmetic. Nonetheless, many philosophers today still work on the relationships between logic and mathematics.

Frege's introduction in predicate logic of quantifiers with variables (like "All x that have a certain property") inspired philosophers to create new symbols to express the logic of modal sentences, which are sentences that express a different modality (way) of being.

For example, "Dogs are animals" is just a regular sentence, but "Dogs are necessarily animals" is a modal claim about how things must be, while "Dogs might possibly be animals" expresses the way things could be.

In the early 1930s, the American philosopher **C. I. Lewis** devised a logic to capture how we think about modal concepts. The sentence "□p" says that dogs *must necessarily be* animals, while the sentence "◊p" says that dogs *might possibly be* animals. Lewis devised five different systems of axioms about necessity (□) and possibility (◊) that expressed various ideas about these concepts.

An **axiom** is a basic rule of a system used to deduce other sentences that will be true for that system. For example, one axiom about necessity states "□p ⇒ p," which says that if the sentence p *must be* true, then that same sentence p *is in fact* true. Another axiom says that this relation doesn't go the other way: "¬(p ⇒ □p)" says that it is not the case that just because p *is* true, p *must be* true. For instance, just because I'm wearing shoes doesn't mean I *must* wear shoes.

In 1951, the Finnish philosopher **Georg Henrik von Wright** used modal symbols to capture the logic of moral obligation. So instead of necessary and possible, Wright's key terms were obligatory, permissible, and forbidden.

Also in the 1950s, New Zealand–born logician **Arthur Prior** developed a logic of time featuring the terms "it will be the case that," "it was the case that," and "it always was that."

In Real Life

In addition to helping us better understand complex issues like metaphysical possibility, moral obligation, and the logic of past and future, logics like these are used to program computers to try to get them to think like we do.

For instance, imagine you're trying to get a computer to understand a story. There are all sorts of relationships between events in the story that can be confusing, and philosophers help computer scientists figure out how to best code our various ways of thinking as algorithms, which are clearly listed procedures that can serve as instructions for a computer.

Taking Sides

Von Wright's moral logic includes the basic axiom "Oa ⇒ Pa," which says that if an action is obligatory, it must be permitted. For example, if I say that helping people is something we are all morally required to do, then I'm committed to also saying that helping people is something we're allowed to do. In other words, "must" implies "may"; "ought" implies "can."

However, even this obvious axiom is questionable. The 5th-century BCE Greek playwright **Sophocles** wrote tragedies in which someone has conflicting moral obligations, like *Antigone*. On the one hand, Antigone must bury her brother, who was killed while rebelling against the government. On the other hand, the government has forbidden her from doing this. So she has two moral obligations that tell her to do opposing things, and they're both binding. This is a tragic type of ethics, where "ought" does not imply "can."

- Try to interpret and reflect on this modal axiom that was part of only one of Lewis's five axiomatic systems: "□p ⇒ □◊p."

- Can you think of another use of modal logic in training a computer to think like we do?

- Do you find logical symbols helpful or just confusing?

CHAPTER 6

Aesthetics: What Is Good Art?

The word "aesthetics" comes from the Greek *aisthetikos* meaning "perception by the senses." To most philosophers, aesthetics means the study of beauty, and some philosophers have argued that understanding beauty has more to do with your mind than your senses.

Some recent philosophers have objected to focusing on beauty in particular, because many good artworks aren't trying to be beautiful. Instead of aesthetics, we could just call this area "the philosophy of art."

WHAT IS BEAUTY?

Why do certain arrangements of color, sound, and movement please us? What makes some faces more appealing than others, some landscapes really striking, and some paintings stop us in our tracks to look at them?

While creating art goes back into prehistory—all the way to cave paintings—treating beauty philosophically is much more recent. In fact, the word "aesthetics" wasn't used until German philosopher **Alexander Baumgarten** first used it in the 18th century. However, some of the ideas these relatively recent philosophers drew on were much older.

WHO ASKED IT?

The 6th-century BCE Greek philosopher **Pythagoras of Samos** is known as a mathematician (you've probably heard of the Pythagorean theorem), but he also studied harmony in music. He and his students figured out that musical pitches have a mathematical relation to each other, such that you can make certain pretty intervals between notes according to the length of a flute, or the tension in a lyre's strings, or how much water is in a jug, or in other ways.

The Pythagoreans thought that the secret of beauty lay in these mathematical relations. We're attracted by things that are organized in a harmonious way.

WHO ANSWERED IT?

Pythagoras influenced Plato, who was suspicious of the senses, and thought that being attracted to beauty is the same as being attracted to the divine Form of goodness. Even though appreciating beauty may start with the senses, like when we hear musical harmony or appreciate a finely carved statue, ultimately, beauty is something only reason can grasp. Perceiving symmetry and harmony can inspire us to think of symmetry and harmony that is too perfect to appear in the world we can perceive.

This introduced a distinction between true beauty and what is merely charming, a shallow experience that Plato thought could be dangerous for us. It's like the difference between food that is good and healthy and food that is just tasty, empty calories.

The 18th-century German philosopher **Christian Freiherr von Wolff** defined beauty as a harmonious relation of the parts of an object. For instance, a mechanical clock has gears that fit together perfectly to precisely tell time. Like Plato, Wolff connected beauty with the enjoyment we get from understanding truth. A great painting, for instance, truly depicts the thing that it's a painting of. However, Wolff also saw beauty as primarily a matter of feelings: Something is beautiful if it has a perfection—like depicting something perfectly—that gives us pleasure.

The late-19th-century Spanish American philosopher **George Santayana** argued that we all have a sense of beauty that grasps certain forms—the arrangement of parts—and materials—like a pretty color or soft fabric—as pleasurable.

In Real Life

Scientific studies have shown that people tend to find symmetrical faces, where the right side and the left side are nearly identical, more beautiful.

The Italian Renaissance painter **Leonardo da Vinci** created a drawing called the *Vitruvian Man* that aimed to show the ideally beautiful proportions of the human body, with parts sized in exact mathematical ratios, just like the frequencies of tones in a musical chord.

The ancient mathematician **Euclid of Alexandria** discovered the golden ratio, a particular mathematical relation (around 1.6 to 1) that we can find in the dimensions of the pyramids, the *Mona Lisa*, and other beautiful objects.

Taking Sides

Do we detect beauty primarily using our senses or our minds? As with epistemology, empiricists like Santayana focus on sense experience, and rationalists like Plato focus on reason.

The practical difference between these positions is that if beauty comes from reason, then people can be wrong in what they find beautiful, because they're not reasoning correctly. Plato thought that people's enjoyment of art can mislead them about what's truly beautiful.

Santayana thought that if you find something beautiful, you can't be wrong about that. However, he also thought that some kinds of artistic appreciation are more sophisticated than others. Santayana thought that enjoying the tone of a singer's voice or the pulse of the drums isn't as deep and affecting an experience as perceiving the structure and harmonies in a symphony. Sensing allows us to enjoy the matter of a work, while thinking is needed to enjoy its form.

Consider This

- What do you think about connecting beauty to mathematics? Do you think your enjoyment of art or nature has anything to do with its parts being proportioned in pleasing ratios? Why or why not?

- Do you think cooking is one of the fine arts? Can something have a beautiful taste or smell? Why or why not?

IS BEAUTY JUST IN THE EYE OF THE BEHOLDER?

The old saying "Beauty is in the eye of the beholder" means that people have different tastes. While arguing about differing tastes in ice cream may not be productive, critics

argue about which pieces of art are great all the time. This suggests that beauty may not be purely objective, just a matter of personal preference.

Is beauty actually in objects, or just in people's minds? Plato and Pythagoras claimed that beauty was objective, but if so, then why do people disagree about beauty as much as they do? Could it make sense to claim that an artwork that people enjoy is not truly enjoyable?

WHO ASKED IT?

The 5th-century BCE Greek Sophist **Protagoras** said that "man is the measure of all things." This means that everything—including not just taste, but also ethics and truth—is relative.

Protagoras didn't leave us any books, but is quoted by various authors who followed him, and he most famously appears as a character arguing with Socrates in one of Plato's works. The two characters interpret some poetry together but mostly argue about ethics. Even if Protagoras was wrong in his wider claim about ethics and truth being relative, the belief that beauty, at least, must be relative has become very common.

WHO ANSWERED IT?

David Hume argued that beauty is not in objects, but is only a feeling in our minds. It's only because this feeling is so calm compared to our emotions that we mistakenly think of the beauty as being actually part of an artwork. Since people have different feelings, we should expect disagreements about beauty.

Nonetheless, Hume thought we are right to say that at least some feelings about beauty are wrong, because beautiful works are ones that could potentially please everyone. It's just that seeing beauty takes practice and attention.

Immanuel Kant agreed that beauty is in our minds, but thought that our minds are all structured basically the same, so beauty is objective anyway. Kant distinguished aesthetic pleasures from other pleasures because the aesthetic ones are "disinterested," which means they don't satisfy our hunger, our vanity, our thirst for thrills, or any other desires. Different perceivers may find different things pleasurable due to their different interests, but truly aesthetic enjoyment, because it is disinterested, can be universal. For example, the beauty of a painting of a bowl of fruit has nothing to do with whether or not you're hungry.

The American philosopher **Nelson Goodman** saw different artists as creating different ways of understanding the world. He thought there are multiple—even conflicting—ways that a work can be beautiful. We shouldn't expect people to all find the same things beautiful, though by learning to understand an artist's style—their artistic language—we can judge whether a particular artwork succeeds.

In Real Life

When you like a song, movie, or other artwork but someone else does not, how do you deal with this? Do you just agree to disagree, or can someone be convinced to change? You might want to show someone you care about that they're missing something. You want them to share in your enjoyment.

Common barriers to enjoying some artwork include not being familiar with its genre ("All country music sounds the same to me") and not being able to relate to something about the style ("Punk rock is too loud! And I don't like their attitudes!").

Taking Sides

Wolff and Kant agreed that beauty lies in something's form: in the arrangement of its parts. But Wolff's example of a watch being beautiful because its parts are arranged to tell time accurately seems to violate Kant's requirement that aesthetic enjoyment be disinterested.

In Kant's view, something's beauty is not related to how useful it is. Aesthetics is therefore very different from ethics. We shouldn't, for instance, judge an artwork based on whether it has a good message that will improve people's behavior. Instead, we merely contemplate a work's structure: its abstract form.

For Wolff, the abstract form of a beautiful object is important, but so is how effectively it achieves its end. Wolff was particularly interested in architecture, and this is an area where form and function are often debated. Can a building really be beautiful if it is constructed in such a way that it will fall down?

Consider This

- Try to think of an occasion when you changed your mind about the quality of some artwork. Was it because you learned something?

- Do you think that tastes are more subjective for some arts than others? For example, is musical taste more subjective than the appreciation of good photography? Why or why not?

DOES ART ALWAYS AIM AT BEAUTY?

Though philosophers for a long time focused on beauty when discussing artworks, there are, of course, other ways that artists try to affect people's emotions. For instance, an artist might show us something deeply disturbing, like the body of someone killed in war.

What makes this good art, and not, for instance, a moral appeal to stop the suffering that war causes? Some philosophers have argued that a good work of art will depict even hideous subjects in a beautiful way. Others have argued that many artworks are aiming at something very different from beauty.

WHO ASKED IT?

Sometime between 200 BCE and 200 CE, the Indian sage **Bharata Muni** composed an encyclopedia of drama and music called the Natyashastra. Instead of considering all art as aiming at beauty, Bharata described various reactions that an artist tries to elicit in an audience, including love, sorrow, anger, disgust, astonishment, and more.

The 1st-century CE Roman author **Longinus** wrote a treatise on good and bad writing called "On the Sublime," in which he argued that the power of attention-catching ideas is the central thing that makes something effectively written, and that the point of a work is to cause the audience to experience intense emotion. An artist can pour out their soul into an artwork, trying to create greatness or express a strong passion. Longinus did not focus on rules for beautiful writing, but instead on a forceful, impressive style, which he called the **sublime**.

WHO ANSWERED IT?

The 18th-century English philosopher **Edmund Burke** brought talk of the sublime to modern aesthetics. Burke recognized that our fear of death is just as powerful a force as beauty is in contemplating something aesthetically. The sublime depicts overwhelming force and vastness, like a mighty storm. Though we would be scared to encounter something like this in the world, a work of art can let us experience it safely.

Friedrich Nietzsche's first book, *The Birth of Tragedy*, discussed the historical transition in ancient Greek art from aiming at the sublime to the beautiful. He called the sublime "Dionysian" after Dionysus, the Greek god of wine, and he called beauty "Apollonian" after Apollo, god of the sun. He identified Plato's attitude with the Apollonian: the idea that beauty has to be pure, eternal, and changeless. Nietzsche thought that this can be inspiring but is fundamentally inhuman. The Dionysian, on the other hand, expresses the real truth of existence according to Nietzsche, which is chaotic and full of constant change.

One of Nietzsche's direct influences was **Arthur Schopenhauer**, who followed Immanuel Kant in distinguishing the world of our experience from the real world, but then argued that we *can* know the real world, and that it—including each of us—is fundamentally a vast, blind, striving, irrational force that he called **Will**, because we can all know it just by reflecting on our own experience of willing (wanting) things. Schopenhauer saw music as especially sublime because it directly expresses this Will.

In Real Life

If you like horror movies, is it because you really like to be scared? Aristotle, in writing about the tragic plays of his time, used the term "catharsis" to describe how watching terrible things happen to people onstage while you sit safely in your seat allows you to flush bad emotions out of your system.

In a story, it might be most beautiful for everything to end happily, with good people rewarded. There's even a satisfying symmetry to bad people being punished. However, a story can be good in the sense of sublime even with an unhappy ending.

Taking Sides

The picture of art as a powerful, almost religious experience was very influential in the Romantic era in early-19th-century Europe, when art was often defined as an expression of an artist's feelings rather than an attempt to capture beauty. However, Nietzsche despised Romanticism, which he saw as shallow and denying the harsh truths of existence.

The English Romantic poet John Keats's poem "Ode on a Grecian Urn" says, "Beauty is truth, truth beauty." This accords with Plato's view of the relation between truth, beauty, and goodness, whereas Nietzsche saw these as very different.

One difficulty here concerns the nature of humanity's most powerful experiences. Extreme ecstasy from art (or from some other source) can make you feel like you're one with the universe, according to the Romantics and Nietzsche. Really intense art, whether intensely beautiful or intensely frightening, attempts to depict the indescribable. We shouldn't expect to be able to clearly distinguish two indescribable experiences.

- Do you enjoy violence or suffering in movies, songs, and stories? Why or why not?

- Do you think that something truly ugly can be beautiful in art? Try to think of an example.

- Can an artwork be *both* beautiful and sublime? Is the sublime just a type of the beautiful? Why or why not?

WHAT COUNTS AS ART?

Discussions of aesthetic experience often take our experiences of nature as an example. Maybe we only ever thought
to make beautiful music because we have the example
of birdsong, or the first inspiration of a photographer or
painter might be seeing something beautiful in nature.

But let's flip this: By appreciating beauty (or the sublime)
in nature, can we transform nature—or whatever object
we're appreciating—into art?

Similarly, if art is whatever an artist creates, does that
mean a sandwich made by an artist is an artwork? Are there
limits to what can count as a work of art?

WHO ASKED IT?

Even though "What is art?" sounds like an extremely basic
question in aesthetics, this is a question that people only really
started to ask at the beginning of the 20th century when
artists began works that were increasingly experimental.

The French painter **Marcel Duchamp** famously submitted a work called *Fountain* to an exhibition in 1917. This was
just a urinal (a toilet) that he found. He didn't make it; he
just bought it. He submitted it anonymously, and then wrote
about it when it was rejected, claiming that as an artist, his
choice to submit it made it art.

WHO ANSWERED IT?

Duchamp's *Fountain* was extraordinarily influential, not
as a physical work—it was, after all, just a toilet—but as a
statement about what art is. Many artists responded: For
instance, the composer **John Cage** wrote "4'33"," which
involved someone sitting in silence at a piano for exactly

4 minutes 33 seconds. **Andy Warhol** created sculptures like *Brillo Box* and *100 Soup Cans*, which duplicated consumer products. Traditional theories of art that emphasize an artwork's form or how it expresses the artist's emotions were dismissive of experimental works like these.

In 1964, the American philosopher **Arthur Danto** outlined what is now called the institutional theory of art, which says that something counts as art if it is created by

an artist and accepted by the art world as art. So displaying *Fountain* as an artwork in a museum makes it an artwork, while the same thing in a restroom isn't.

Monroe Beardsley, a contemporary of Danto's, agreed that we should look at an artist's intentions, but stressed that these intentions have to include satisfying someone's aesthetic interest. So if *Fountain* was really just created as a comment about art, and not to be contemplated as an artwork, then it shouldn't be included.

In 1979, the American philosopher **Jerrold Levinson** gave a historical theory of art, which states that an artwork has to be related to what has been treated as art in the past. What works have people contemplated and been emotionally affected by? Any creation similar to those counts as art.

In Real Life

Art has come a long way in the last century, and we probably have different cases than *Fountain* in mind when we're asking whether something is art. Can a really well-designed shoe or phone be art? Clearly dance is an art, but can you move with such grace that even the way you walk should be considered an art? A chef can be an artist by creating innovative, pleasing-looking, and delicious dishes, but what about a chemist who likewise mixes interesting ingredients? Maybe art is less about creating a product than adopting an artistic attitude toward the world.

Taking Sides

The idea of **formalism in aesthetics** states that you can know something is an artwork just by experiencing the work. You don't have to know anything about where that artwork came from, which means that even a particularly beautiful stick that someone found and presented as art could count, but *Fountain* would not. Probably all of the classical philosophers of aesthetics would agree with this.

Danto claimed, however, that you could have two works that are identical, and yet one of them that was created by an artist would count as art, and another that was created for some other reason would not. Warhol's creations are a good example here, because unlike *Fountain*, these were sculptures and paintings that Warhol created, even though they reproduced images that were originally created for commercial purposes. Warhol was asking us to look afresh at these things and think about commercialism.

Consider This

- Stop and just listen to what's around you right now. Can you by an act of will perceive that sound as musical?

- Do you think that the artist's intention or character matters when you're experiencing a work of art? Why or why not?

- Do you think *Fountain* is art? Is it *good* art?

CAN ART MAKE ME A BETTER (OR WORSE) PERSON?

Judgments of artistic quality, like judgments of ethics, are normative. This means they don't just describe, but also evaluate. So how do judgments about beauty or artistic quality relate to ethical judgments?

Kant thought that aesthetic judgments are totally independent from ethics. But of course every artwork involves more than just abstract forms to be contemplated disinterestedly: Art is a powerful tool for getting people to care about things, from characters to political causes. Given how central movies, TV, music, and other artworks are to most of our daily lives, philosophers have wondered what kind of arts are good for us.

WHO ASKED IT?

Daoist artists inspired by Laozi created images depicting and expressing living in harmony with nature. For instance, **Wu Boli**'s 14th-century painting *Dragon Pine* (a depiction of which can be seen on page 121) teaches the Daoist virtues of grace, endurance, and balance. This is typical of much religious art across faiths: couple a positive message with a calming sensory experience that encourages quiet contemplation and joy.

Plato's view equating true beauty with goodness was influential in inspiring devotional artworks in the Judeo-Christian world, but his own view of art was much less positive. Ancient Greeks—along with most philosophers up to the 19th century—thought a good painting was one that accurately depicted its subject matter. It was only when photography was introduced and could do this flawlessly that painters had to rethink this goal. Even music, which seems more abstract, was, according to Aristotle, an imitation of human movement and emotions.

For Plato, our world is already an imitation of the true world, so art is an imitation of an imitation, and artists are essentially liars. Plato considered many of the stories of the Greek gods to be sacrilege, depicting gods as poorly behaved humans.

WHO ANSWERED IT?

Eighteenth-century Romantic philosophers like **Friedrich von Schlegel** thought that aesthetics was absolutely central for how we should live. Schlegel thought that poetry and philosophy are really the same thing and that making the world more poetic should be a central concern of politics, ethics, and even science.

Even though Nietzsche disliked Romanticism, his whole conception of ethics was based around making your life into a work of art. He thought that both ethics and aesthetics are a matter of what we value: They're both about wanting a certain kind of world.

Schopenhauer thought that aesthetic experience was a matter of understanding that you are really the universal Will underlying all of nature. Since, according to Schopenhauer's metaphysics, *everyone* is also this same Will, aesthetics gives an important way to understand our connection to other people, and this is necessary for ethics. Art makes us compassionate.

Kierkegaard saw aesthetics, ethics, and religion as three different ways of valuing things, with aesthetics being the least sophisticated of these. He thought that being concerned with what you experience through your senses makes you selfish and shallow, and that this concern should be overcome—though not entirely abandoned, because when art is put into perspective, it can serve higher goals. For instance, Kierkegaard's writings about religion were themselves very artistic.

Kierkegaard and Nietzsche are often considered early existentialists. Existentialism stresses our freedom to create ourselves, and many existentialist philosophers wrote novels, plays, and other literary works. The French novelist **Albert Camus**, for instance, saw life as fundamentally absurd. We want the world to be orderly, and our activities to fit in harmoniously with this orderly world, but none of this is true. Art can help us accept and cope with this reality.

The early-20th-century American pragmatist **John Dewey** argued that art has to do with more than artworks in museums, and is about living in a vibrant, fully engaged way.

Many 20th-century critics have argued that modern entertainment is bad for us. For example, the Marxist philosopher **Theodor W. Adorno** argued that popular songs and shows are manufactured to make us slaves to our capitalist economy. The Canadian philosopher **Marshall McLuhan** criticized the bite-size form in which we receive information. His slogan "The medium is the message" means that the way we receive information sets limits on what kind of information we can receive.

In Real Life

Many people use music as a soundtrack to their lives. By playing songs in the background, they make the world feel a particular way.

Plato thought that certain kinds of music were bad for the human spirit and should be banned, while other kinds were uplifting.

Do you feel like having a particular type of soundtrack can make you a better or worse person? What does it say about you if you, for instance, always listen to sad music, or angry music, or music that sounds very experimental?

Taking Sides

Irony is a technique in artistic writing where you don't just say what you mean. Maybe you say the opposite of what you mean (like sarcasm), or maybe the relation between what you say and what you mean is left purposely unclear.

Irony was used in philosophy as far back as Plato. The word *ironia* in ancient Greek means pretending to be ignorant. It's not always clear when Socrates is stating what he really believes or just trying to get us to think about an idea.

Romantics like Schlegel used irony to expose the limits of knowledge. Ironically discussing a philosophical theory lets you explore it without fully committing to it. Schlegel used irony to show that what he was saying was only one of an infinite number of perspectives.

Kierkegaard also used irony, publishing many works under different names, taking on different characters and writing from their perspectives. However, irony, for him, was about putting distance between yourself and the absurd, mundane world to be closer to what he saw as the best perspective: God's.

Consider This

- Do you think art has a role in making us better people? If so, is just experiencing art enough, or do you have to actually create art?

- What do you think is the relationship between what is ethically good and what is aesthetically good? Are they the same thing?

CHAPTER 7

Political Philosophy: How Should We Organize Society?

T he word "politics" comes from the ancient Greek *polis*, which is what the ancient Greeks called their city-states. Each polis was politically independent, with its own government. (There was no central government for all of Greece.)

On the one hand, political philosophy is a subdivision of ethics, addressing not how we should act individually, but how we should act together. On the other hand, political philosophy is an engineering question: What sorts of laws can efficiently organize people to live together well?

WHAT'S THE PURPOSE OF GOVERNMENT?

Why even have a government? Why not just live by yourself in the middle of the woods? While some people find this a desirable way to live, there are obvious advantages to living near other people. When we do live together, there

are inevitably disputes over who gets to have land, property, privilege, and respect. Is the purpose of government just to manage these disputes? To help everyone live as well as possible? A political state means using force to make sure people follow the law. Is that something we want, or something we must tolerate?

WHO ASKED IT?

Each Greek city-state could have its own type of government, and this led philosophers in Greece, more than philosophers in other places, to question what a government should be for. Aristotle claimed that we are political animals. This means that public life—engaging with people in political activities—is part of the good life for us. We all need systems and rules to help us peacefully and productively relate to each other, and so governments naturally develop to address this need. Aristotle evaluated the different kinds of government he knew of to see which ones met human needs most effectively.

WHO ANSWERED IT?

Thomas Hobbes argued like Aristotle that government is a natural thing we all want, whether we admit it or not. Hobbes used the phrase "nasty, brutish, and short" to describe what the world would be like without any kind of government. Nothing would stop people from constantly hurting each other. It's in our interest to give up our abilities to hurt each other and instead put all disputes in the hands of a ruler. Hobbes called this deal the **social contract**. Even if we've never said out loud, "I agree to be governed," Hobbes thought that our human nature commits us to such an agreement. Interestingly, the ruler is not someone who signed the contract. Hobbes thought that a world without government would be so bad that we would all agree to surrender all our rights to the leader, who should have absolute power over the rest of us.

John Locke liked the idea of a social contract, but thought that the ruler should be restricted by the contract, too. Locke argued that there's a law of nature that ethically requires us to respect each other's lives, liberty, and property. The government's job is to make sure those rights are respected, and if the government violates those rights, the citizens must replace the government with a better one.

The 18th-century French philosopher **Jean-Jacques Rousseau** argued that the purpose of government is to enforce the will of the people, which aims at what is best for us as a group: equality.

In Real Life

Do you think that by living in your society and being protected by its laws, you've made a deal that requires you to obey the law yourself? The idea of a social contract of this sort goes all the way back to Socrates.

In Plato's dialogue *Crito*, Socrates has just been unjustly sentenced to death. He is offered the opportunity to escape, but says this would violate his duty to his polis. He has accepted the benefits of living in Athens all his life, and going against it now would be wrong, even if it made a mistake in condemning him.

Taking Sides

Locke and Rousseau agreed that the point of government is to protect human rights, but disagreed about what those rights include. Locke thought that the right to private property is natural. We naturally own our own bodies, so we can legitimately claim to own things we have created and land that we have put labor into by farming or otherwise cultivating. However, people shouldn't hoard property they can't make use of.

For Rousseau, private property is merely a social construction, not something natural. Governments run by the rich tend to protect their wealth, but a truly representative government should just do what the will of the people dictates and protect their interests. While this doesn't mean getting rid of property, it does mean property is not a fundamental right. Property should exist and be protected by the government only if doing this is in the interest of the people.

Consider This

- Do you think you have the obligation to obey an unjust law? Why or why not? Try to think of an example.

- Which do you think would be worse: a terrible government, or no government at all? What do you think the world would be like without governments?

IS DEMOCRACY THE BEST KIND OF GOVERNMENT?

The great story in the history of political philosophy is the gradual acceptance of the idea that some people shouldn't have total power over others. You're not going to find too many philosophers today who argue that we should have kings or a permanent ruling class that enslaves the rest of us. But is **democracy**—where the people vote for laws, and the majority wins—the best way to make laws that respect people's right to rule themselves?

How much democracy is enough? Should we vote on every law ourselves, or just vote for representatives who then will make the laws?

WHO ASKED IT?

"Democracy" comes from a word in ancient Greek that means "rule of the people." Athens was known as a democracy, but we should keep in mind that only free adult men who had completed military training—about 10 to 20 percent of the Athenian people—could actually vote for laws or be part of a jury.

Given that an Athenian jury voted to put Socrates to death, his followers Plato and Aristotle had doubts that democracy was the best way to ensure wise governance. Plato (through the character of Socrates) mused in his dialogue *The Republic* that it would make the most sense for only wise and virtuous people to rule: philosopher kings.

WHO ANSWERED IT?

Plato's student Aristotle experienced the final years of Athenian democracy as well as the period after Athens was conquered by the kingdom of Macedonia, when he worked directly for the new king. He was in a good position to evaluate which kind of government would result in the most justice and fairness for all its citizens. Aristotle agreed with Plato that the most virtuous should rule, but recognized that this is much easier said than done. He recommended a constitution that would restrict the power of whoever is in charge, and also thought that people should be able to change this constitution to adapt to new situations. Aristotle saw rule by the many as a fragile form of government, very likely to result in injustice as the poor take over.

John Stuart Mill, as a utilitarian, believed that the function of government is to make the most people happy and reduce suffering. He argued, for instance, that women should have the right to vote. However, he also warned of the "tyranny of the majority," which means that in a democracy, it's likely that people will vote in the interests of their own group instead of for what's good for everyone. Therefore, minority groups are likely to be harmed or ignored.

James Madison, one of the authors of the US Constitution, had Mill's warning clearly in mind when he argued that America should be a democratic republic, where people would vote for those virtuous enough to respect everyone's rights.

In Real Life

In a true democracy, everyone would vote on everything. This means that everyone would need to be educated about every issue they're asked to vote on, from land use to trade policy to which scientific efforts deserve funding.

But none of us really has time to learn about all that. We inevitably receive advice from people we see as experts in various areas, or whose judgment we trust enough that we think those people will find and learn from the appropriate experts.

Do we want to spend time constantly researching and voting, or just elect those people whose judgment we respect?

Taking Sides

Rousseau thought, on the one hand, that only a true democracy could actually express the will of the people. But on the other hand, he thought this would only be feasible for small groups that are liable to be conquered by larger ones, that rich people are not likely to let themselves be ruled by the many, and that democracies are liable to break out into civil wars. So he wasn't very hopeful about democracy, or about the ability of any government to truly represent the common good.

John Dewey was optimistic that people can be educated to be effective citizens in a democracy, and that democracy is the only form of government in which we can develop fully as human beings. Through good education, every single one of us can become worthy of democracy, able to make better decisions about the common good than any representative.

- A good constitution is supposed to protect minorities from the tyranny of the majority. Do you think the US Constitution does this well enough? Why or why not?

- Think of an example where voting for what's best for everyone overall would mean voting to give up some advantage you currently have. Which way would you vote?

WHAT IS JUSTICE?

Lots of people argue about **social justice**, but what is it, exactly? What do people owe each other, and what should government be doing to make sure that they get it? Justice plays a key role in our criminal laws: When a law is broken, we want justice to be done. But justice also has to do more generally with how society is organized. Who gets to be in control? Who gets to have the most stuff, the most responsibility, and the most respect? This is often called distributive justice: What's the fairest way to pass out goods?

WHO ASKED IT?

The Code of Hammurabi gave us the first historical principle of justice, "an eye for an eye," but the idea that kicked off our modern conception of justice came from the Code of Justinian in 529 CE.

Justinian I was the emperor of the Byzantine Empire (the eastern half of the Roman Empire), and his code defined justice as "the constant and perpetual will to render each his due." It's not enough for people to be punished for misdeeds. Justice also requires that we all get whatever we deserve. But what do people deserve, and how should government promote this?

WHO ANSWERED IT?

All the social contract theorists I mentioned earlier were giving answers to who rightfully gets to rule and what the rulers owe to the people. Locke and Rousseau both stressed that everyone should be treated equally by laws, and that they should have a say in what those laws are, and, therefore, what that society considers just laws and punishments.

Rousseau went further to reject the inequality, which he said was a result of society. However, he still wasn't fully egalitarian, which is the idea that everyone is equal and so deserves all the same goods that life has to offer. Thinkers like **Martin Luther King Jr.** traced **egalitarianism** directly back to passages in the Bible that say we are all equal in God's eyes.

The 19th-century philosopher **Karl Marx** believed in egalitarianism, and argued that justice means each person should contribute to society according to their ability and receive goods according to their needs.

The 20th-century American philosopher **John Rawls** said that we can know the fair way to hand out goods by imagining that we're setting up a society without knowing what role we as individuals will have in it. He thought we would therefore want to make the poorest people as well off as possible, and that inequality should be permitted if it raises that lowest place.

The Jamaican American philosopher **Charles Mills** argued that we can't just think in abstract terms about how to justly organize society, but have to actively undo the effects of past injustice.

In Real Life

Black Lives Matter protesters have argued that despite the United States' official law that everyone should be treated equally, that's not the way it works in reality. They claim that the country's policies in policing and courts lead to more Black people being harassed and killed by police and more being imprisoned, with harsher sentences than those given to white people convicted of the same crimes. Do you agree that a difference in how a law affects different groups of people is good evidence that that law—or how it is being interpreted and enforced—is unjust? Why or why not?

Taking Sides

John Rawls's contemporary **Robert Nozick** replied that the whole idea of society handing out goods makes no sense. Governments do not initially own everything, and it's unjust for them to take goods from the people who own them to redistribute them to others. Instead of evaluating how much people have, Nozick thought we should evaluate how these goods were acquired. If no theft, lying, or other bad means were involved, then there is justice in the current way goods are distributed, even if there is great inequality.

Marx argued that the initial arrangement of private property is always the result of theft, of powerful people taking what they can and then creating laws that say they own what they do justly. He also thought that how goods are acquired in a capitalist society is always unjust, because workers are forced to work for the rich. They have no meaningful realistic alternative, and so they aren't free.

- What kinds of equality do you think society should be striving for?

- Do you think that justice means making up for past injustice? How far in the past does this extend? Should it matter to us now if someone stole someone else's land many years ago? Why or why not?

WHAT MAKES A GOOD LEADER?

In nearly every kind of government, someone has responsibilities that can greatly affect the lives of others, so philosophers have thought a lot about what qualities a good leader should have. This question is tied to virtue ethics—how can I be a good person?—but introduces the element of managing power. Do any of the same lessons for good leadership apply both to emperors and to being a leader on a class project? Reflecting on good leadership can help us understand the difficulties built into organizing society and making positive changes in the world.

WHO ASKED IT?

Confucius's philosophy aimed to create wise leaders who would help their nation be in harmony with the universe. By being virtuous and always doing their duty, leaders serve as models for their followers. Confucius advised leaders to cultivate a love of learning, to be modest, to put all their efforts toward setting a good example, to be compassionate by imagining themselves in another's place, and to never use power unjustly.

Also in the 6th century BCE, **Sunzi** (a.k.a. Sun Tzu), in *The Art of War*, stressed that an effective leader will be humane even while treating people as tools to achieve their goal of winning.

WHO ANSWERED IT?

Plato described ideal leaders in his book *The Republic*: These should be philosopher kings who care only about virtue and not about power. A tyrant, according to Plato, is someone who is actually enslaved by their own desires.

Marcus Aurelius Antoninus, a Stoic Roman emperor in the 2nd century CE, advised that leaders should be careful to always lead with seriousness and justice. They should never be swept up by emotion, always be truthful, and follow the will of nature by living in a straightforward, simple, healthy manner.

In *The Prince*, the 16th-century Italian philosopher **Niccolò Machiavelli** advised rulers to be ruthless in taking and keeping power. They shouldn't be restrained by morality. It is better for them to be feared than loved. However, for a society to last long term, Machiavelli recommended building institutions and passing laws that cast the leader as a defender of law, order, and tradition.

The Dutch Catholic humanist **Erasmus** responded to Machiavelli's book with his book The *Education of a Christian Prince*, in which he claimed that a leader is the servant of his people and should serve with honor.

Montesquieu (a.k.a. Charles-Louis de Secondat, baron de Montesquieu) argued that the kind of government determines what kind of leader will be effective. A king should create as free and humane a country as possible so that its people will serve out of loyalty and honor, while in a democracy, the primary stabilizing characteristic is virtue: A good leader must take the public trust seriously and influence all citizens to do the same.

Think about how **American presidents are evaluated.** Most Americans want their presidents to not just *be* good, but also *look* good. In the United States' democracy, we realize that if a politician we support can't appeal to lots of other people, then that politician will not continue to win.

This leads us to evaluate potential politicians in a strange way, asking not just "Do I support what this person believes in?" but also "Do I feel like this politician is appealing enough to win?"

What do you think Confucius or Erasmus would say about this way of evaluating potential leaders?

Taking Sides

Do virtuous people finish last? This is the question that the term "Machiavellian" generally raises. While Plato argued that a good leader should ignore popular opinion if it goes against what is right, Machiavelli thought that a leader who chooses principle over popularity won't last very long. If possible, he said, just continue the policies of the previous office-holder exactly, as that will upset the least number of people possible, so you'll have a long reign.

But Plato's radical suggestions in *The Republic* for how government should be set up—which include full gender equality along with some weird proposals like kicking all the poets out of the city—suggest that his philosopher kings would be anything but conservative. They would absolutely do what they thought was best for the country, even if it was likely to anger many people who were happy with the current state of things.

Consider This

- Do you think the best leaders listen to what their followers want or just do what they think to be right?

- What do you think it means to lead "in accordance with nature" as Confucius and Aurelius recommend?

- Do the pressures of democracy mean that none of our leaders can be virtuous? Why or why not?

WHAT ARE HUMAN RIGHTS?

The idea of rights derives from the moral question "What is the right thing to do?" In this sense, it's one of the oldest questions in political philosophy, because all of the world's ethical traditions provide rules or virtues for the right way to deal with others, and especially the right way to rule. But the idea of a *right* as something that an individual person can possess, which means no one should be allowed to treat that person in certain ways, is a newer idea, and originally only applied to the powerful. If human rights apply to everyone, what do they include?

WHO ASKED IT?

The **Magna Carta** was an agreement from 1215 that put limits on what the king could do to English nobles. Later thinkers like the founders of the United States took inspiration from the idea of natural rights to argue that the power of government should be restricted to only certain kinds of actions. People have the right to have a voice in government decisions, and there are certain limits on people's control over themselves that no government should restrict, unless the person has committed a crime, and even then, the accused has the right to be treated fairly by the law.

Historians point to ancient documents from Egypt, Persia, Greece, and elsewhere as early examples of human rights, but like the Magna Carta, these largely had to do with particular legal arrangements: that some group of people should not be forced by some specified other people to change their religion, or should not kill prisoners of war, or are allowed to vote in the assembly.

Religion was an early concern of human rights efforts, with laws about religious tolerance going back even to 6th-century Iran under **Cyrus the Great** and to the 3rd century BCE in ancient India under the Buddhist emperor **Ashoka**.

WHO ANSWERED IT?

An ongoing issue in debates about rights is whether they are natural or merely political, meaning granted by individual governments. The idea of a natural right to life goes back to **Mahavira**, the 6th-century BCE founder of the Indian religion of Jainism. In the modern age, John Locke declared that we have the God-given rights of life, liberty, and property.

Jeremy Bentham, by contrast, called natural rights "nonsense on stilts." He thought that while there are objectively correct moral principles (his utilitarianism), rights are something that governments grant. This means that they are matters of ongoing negotiation, and no right is absolute, because laws can be changed and always need to be interpreted. Claiming that something is a natural right is just a claim that something *should be* respected as a legal right.

John Stuart Mill, another utilitarian, thought that in general, government should seek to maximize human welfare. However, he didn't think that this calculation should be newly performed for every single proposed act by the government. For instance, if you're considering whether to prohibit certain kinds of speech that most people really hate, then outlawing that seems like it would be the right thing to do, but Mill saw rights—including the right of free speech—as the best way of applying utilitarian ethics to law. He argued that government should only act to prevent people from harming each other. Speech and other forms of self-expression should be protected, because these are needed for people to flourish and will result in the best society over the long run. He thought that good ideas will always eventually gain acceptance over bad ideas.

Edmund Burke, arguing against the French Revolution, said that rights need societies to make them into real protections for people, and that government is actually a fragile achievement that shouldn't be overthrown. Like Hobbes, he thought that chaos is much worse than oppression. Burke advocated conservatism, which means retaining the good parts of past society. He thought progress should be gradual. There can therefore be no absolute natural rights that society must enforce, but instead a gradual process of seeing how much freedom the government can grant people without society falling apart.

The current American philosopher **Elizabeth S. Anderson** has argued that rights shouldn't be a concern just of governments, but also of employers, who have a great deal of direct control over the lives of their workers.

In Real Life

Until recently, it was widely accepted in the United States that we have no rights when the government calls on us for military service. Do you think government should have the power to command you to join the military and to kill—and maybe die—on their orders? Why or why not?

Millions of people are effectively imprisoned by poverty, with very limited life choices. Anderson, Marx, and others claim that employers as a class greatly restrict the freedom of those who work for them. Is our system of employment also a case of society demanding that we pitch in? Why or why not?

Taking Sides

Both Democrats and **Republicans in American politics claim to be working to protect human rights. Republicans are currently the conservative party, which, as with Burke's conservatism, means they focus on conserving the things about our society that they think have worked. This includes maximum freedom for employers, who conservative economists claim are responsible for making America prosperous.**

Democrats, as the progressive party, focus more on fixing problems they see in our system, including people left behind by our prosperity and the inequalities that have resulted from our economy.

These parties disagree about what rights we really have and what the government should do to secure them. As Burke argued, no right is real unless there are systems in place to support it. This means free speech requires public forums where people can be heard, for example.

Consider This

- Some people claim that without the right to own weapons, no other rights are safe. What do you think are our most important rights?

- Is free speech just a matter of not being censored by the government, or do you think this right can be violated by other organizations or individual people?

Philosopher Guide

All dates are in the common era (CE) unless indicated as before common era (BCE). A "ca." stands for "circa," meaning "about" (we don't know exactly when most of the ancient figures lived).

Adorno, Theodor W. (1903–1969): Born in Germany, taught in the US. Focused on social critique and music.

Anaxagoras (ca. 500–428 BCE): Pre-Socratic metaphysician and astronomer born in what is now Turkey.

Anaximenes of Miletus (ca. 586–526 BCE): Pre-Socratic metaphysician from Turkey who proposed that everything is made of air.

Anderson, Elizabeth S. (1959–): Professor at the University of Michigan focusing on political philosophy, ethics, and feminist philosophy.

Anscombe, Elizabeth (1919–2001): British analytic philosopher who focused on mind, ethics, logic, language, and action.

Anselm of Canterbury, Saint (1033–1109): Italian Catholic monk called "the father of scholasticism," i.e., church-associated philosophy before the Enlightenment.

Aristotle (384–322 BCE): Greek student of Plato who wrote across all philosophical and scientific disciplines.

Ashoka (ca. 304–232 BCE): Indian emperor of the Maurya Dynasty. Converted to Buddhism after witnessing numerous war deaths.

Augustine of Hippo, Saint (354–430): North African theologian who came up with the idea of original sin.

Bacon, Francis (1561–1626): English statesman and philosopher who developed the scientific method and wrote about law and theology.

Baumgarten, Alexander Gottlieb (1714–1762): German philosopher who launched the modern study of aesthetics, applying that word to beauty.

Beardsley, Monroe (1915–1985): Taught at Swarthmore College and Temple University in Pennsylvania, writing primarily on aesthetics.

Benedict, Ruth (1887–1948): American anthropologist most famous for her 1934 book *Patterns of Culture*.

Bentham, Jeremy (1748–1832): English philosopher and jurist who founded utilitarianism: the greatest happiness principle in ethics.

Berkeley, George (1685–1753): Irish English bishop who wrote about epistemology and metaphysics; known as an idealist.

Bharata Muni (ca. 200 BCE to 200 CE): Indian sage thought to have written an encyclopedic treatise about drama and music called the Natyashastra.

Boethius (477–524): Roman senator who wrote *The Consolation of Philosophy* while awaiting execution. Translated Plato and Aristotle into Latin.

Burke, Edmund (1729–1797): Conservative English statesman, economist, and philosopher who wrote about politics and aesthetics.

Cage, John (1912–1992): American experimental composer and philosopher who challenged definitions of what music includes.

Camus, Albert (1913–1960): French author who wrote *The Stranger*, *The Plague*, and other novels, plays, and essays.

Carnap, Rudolf (1891–1970): Austrian philosopher who moved to the US during World War II. Focused on logic and epistemology.

Carneades (ca. 214–129 BCE): Greek skeptic who focused on epistemology to refute existing philosophical schools.

Chrysippus (ca. 279–206 BCE): Cicilian-born Greek logician known as the second founder of Stoicism (after Zeno).

Cicero, Marcus Tullius (ca. 106–43 BCE): Roman statesman and philosophical skeptic known as a great orator.

Confucius, also called Kongzi (ca. 551–179 BCE): Chinese philosopher, poet, and politician whose sayings were collected in a book now called *Analects*.

Constant, Benjamin (1767–1830): Swiss French political thinker and activist who wrote on politics and love.

Cyrus the Great (ca. 600–530 BCE): Founded the first Persian Empire, which spanned from Central Asia to the Mediterranean Sea.

Danto, Arthur (1924–2013): American art critic for *The Nation* who taught philosophy at Columbia University.

Democritus (ca. 460–370 BCE): Pre-Socratic cosmologist who (with his mentor Leucippus) invented the atomic theory of the universe.

Descartes, René (1596–1650): French philosopher, mathematician, and scientist who wrote on epistemology and philosophical method.

Dewey, John (1859–1952): American pragmatist who wrote about politics and art, and was especially influential in education.

Dignaga (ca. 480–540): One of the founders of Indian Buddhist logic and epistemology.

Dostoyevsky, Fyodor
(1821–1881): Russian existentialist novelist who wrote *Crime and Punishment, The Brothers Karamazov,* and other works.

Duchamp, Marcel
(1887–1968): French painter, sculptor, and conceptual artist who challenged traditional definitions of art.

Einstein, Albert (1879–1955): German-born theoretical physicist who revolutionized physics.

Epictetus (ca. 50–135): Turkish-born Roman Stoic philosopher who taught that we should accept external events beyond our control.

Epicurus (341–270 BCE): Greek founder of Epicureanism, which preached simple living in a material world.

Erasmus, Desiderius
(ca. 1466–1536): Dutch Catholic theologian best known for his ethical treatise *In Praise of Folly.*

Euclid of Alexandria
(ca. 325–270 BCE): Ancient Greek mathematician who founded a basic system of geometry.

Frege, Gottlob (1848–1925): German logician and mathematician who founded modern logic with his predicate calculus.

Galen (ca. 129–216): Greek physician who did influential work in anatomy and other medical disciplines.

Gautama, Akshapada: Indian philosopher who wrote the Nyaya-sutras, texts on epistemology and logic. (May have lived sometime between the 6th century BCE and the 2nd century CE.)

Gautama, Siddhartha (the Buddha): Religious leader in ancient India in the 6th or 5th century BCE.

al-Ghazali, Abu Hamid (ca. 1058–1111): Iranian theologian who revived Islamic philosophy and focused on epistemology, law, and mysticism.

Gödel, Kurt Friedrich
(1906–1978): Austrian mathematician and logician famous for his incompleteness theorem about axiomatic systems in mathematics.

Goodman, Nelson
(1906–1998): Harvard professor and art dealer who wrote about epistemology, metaphysics, and art.

Hammurabi (ca. 1810–1750 BCE): King of Babylonia who is believed to have issued the Code of Hammurabi.

Heraclitus (ca. 535–475 BCE): Turkish-born pre-Socratic cosmologist who wrote that everything is fire and structured by logos (reason).

Herodotus (ca. 484–425 BCE): Greek historian and geographer who wrote *Histories*, declaring "custom is king."

Hobbes, Thomas (1588–1679): A founder of English political philosophy who also wrote about science and law.

Hume, David (1711–1776): A Scottish philosopher, historian, and economist who wrote about all aspects of human nature.

Ibn Sina, also called Avicenna (980–1037): Persian philosopher born in what is now Uzbekistan who combined Aristotle's thoughts with Islam.

Ishvarakrisna (ca. 350 CE): The supposed author of the Samkhya-karika, which established the Samkyha philosophy of epistemology.

James, William (1842-1910): American psychologist who helped found pragmatism and experimental psychology.

Joachim, Harold H.
(1868–1938): A British idealist (everything is really ideas) who argued for the coherence theory of truth.

Justinian I (482-565): Byzantine emperor whose code of laws provided one of the earliest definitions of justice.

Kant, Immanuel (1724–1804): German philosopher who wrote on epistemology, ethics, and aesthetics and thought metaphysics was impossible.

Keats, John (1795–1821): English Romantic poet who wrote "Ode on a Grecian Urn" and "Ode to a Nightingale."

Kierkegaard, Søren (1813–1855): Danish theologian, poet, and social critic, considered the first existentialist philosopher.

King, Martin Luther, Jr. (1929–1968): American Baptist minister and nonviolent activist for civil rights.

Kuhn, Thomas Samuel (1922–1996): Professor at Harvard and Berkeley who wrote *The Structure of Scientific Revolutions.*

Lakatos, Imré (1922–1974): Hungarian philosopher of science and mathematics

known for his concept of a scientific research program.

Laozi, also called Lao-tzu (ca. 571 BCE): The reputed author of the *Daodejing* and founder of Daoism.

Leonardo da Vinci (1452–1519): Italian Renaissance painter, sculptor, inventor, and engineer who painted *The Last Supper.*

Levinson, Jerrold (1948–): Philosophy professor at the University of Maryland, College Park, who writes on aesthetics.

Lewis, Clarence Irving (1883–1964): American pragmatist who wrote on logic, ethics, and epistemology.

Locke, John (1632–1704): English philosopher and physician who wrote on epistemology and politics.

Longinus (ca. 1–25): Name given to the author of *On the Sublime.* Often called Pseudo-Longinus to distinguish him from other famous Romans of the same name.

Luther, Martin (1483–1546): German priest who protested Catholic practices and kicked off the Protestant Reformation.

Machiavelli, Niccolò (1469–1527): Italian diplomat and historian who advised rulers, most famously via his book *The Prince.*

MacIntyre, Alasdair (1929–): Scottish American philosopher who writes on moral and political philosophy, including *After Virtue.*

Madison, James (1751–1836): The fourth president of the United States who helped draft the Constitution and co-wrote the *Federalist Papers.*

Mahavira (ca. 540–468 BCE): Indian Jainist religious figure whose teachings were collected as the Jain Agamas.

Maimonides, Moses (1135–1204): Medieval Jewish Torah scholar, astronomer, and physician who wrote *Guide for the Perplexed.*

Malebranche, Nicolas (1638–1715): French Catholic priest who wrote about rationalist epistemology and metaphysics.

Marcus Aurelius Antoninus (121–180): Roman emperor and Stoic considered to be a "philosopher king."

Marx, Karl (1818-1883): German philosopher and economist who devised and promoted Communism.

McLuhan, Marshall (1911–1980): Canadian philosopher who studied media theory and coined the phrase "The medium is the message."

Mill, John Stuart (1806–1873): English politician, economist, and philosopher who wrote about ethics, logic, and reforming politics.

Mills, Charles (1951–2021): Jamaican American philosopher who wrote about political philosophy and race in *The Racial Contract* (1997).

Montesquieu, full name Charles-Louis de Secondat, baron de Montesquieu (1689–1755): French political philosopher and historian who popularized the idea of separation of powers.

Moore, G.E. (1873–1958): English philosopher who helped found analytic philosophy and wrote about ethics and epistemology.

Murdoch, Iris (1919–1999): Irish/British novelist and philosopher who wrote *Under the Net*.

Nagarjuna (ca. 150–250): Indian Mahayana Buddhist saint who founded the Madhyamaka ("middle way") school and preached emptiness.

Nagel, Thomas (1937–): American philosopher who taught political philosophy and ethics at New York University.

Newton, Isaac (1643–1727): English astronomer, physicist, and mathematician who invented calculus and Newtonian physics.

Nietzsche, Friedrich (1844–1900): German classics professor and cultural critic who philosophized about ethics, art, and psychology.

Nozick, Robert (1938–2002): American philosopher who wrote about libertarian political philosophy among other topics.

Origen of Alexandria, (ca. 184–253): Early Christian theologian who wrote over 2,000 treatises and invented hermeneutics.

Paley, William (1743–1805): English utilitarian clergyman and philosopher who formulated a version of the design argument for God.

Peirce, Charles Sanders (1839–1914): American logician, mathematician, and scientist called the father of pragmatism.

Plato (ca. 428–348 BCE): Athenian philosopher who wrote dialogues about all philosophical subjects, featuring his teacher Socrates.

Popper, Karl Raimund (1902-1994): Austrian British philosopher and social commentator who wrote about science and politics.

Prior, Arthur (1914-1969): New Zealand logician and philosopher who founded tense (temporal) logic.

Protagoras (ca. 490–420 BCE): Greek pre-Socratic Sophist who said, "Man is the measure of all things."

Ptolemy (ca. 100–170): Egyptian mathematician and astronomer who argued that Earth is the center of the universe.

Pyrrho (ca. 360–270 BCE): Greek founder of skepti-cism (Pyrrhonism); we only know his writings via the work of philosopher Sextus Empiricus.

Pythagoras of Samos (ca. 570–495 BCE): Greek mathematician who

founded an ascetic school and preached the immortal-ity of the soul.

Rawls, John (1921-2002): American political philoso-pher in the liberal tradition who wrote about justice as fairness.

Rousseau, Jean-Jacques (1712-1778): French phi-losopher, novelist, and composer who wrote about political philosophy and education.

Russell, Bertrand (1872-1970): British phi-losopher who wrote about mathematics, logic, episte-mology, and politics.

Ryle, Gilbert (1900-1976): British philosopher who argued against Cartesian mind-body dualism in *The Concept of Mind*.

Santayana, George (1862-1952): Spanish American philosopher and cultural critic who wrote mostly about aesthetics and religion.

Sartre, Jean-Paul (1905-1980): French

existentialist philosopher and political theorist who also wrote novels and plays.

Schlegel, Friedrich von (1772–1829): Poet, classics scholar, and philosopher who kicked off the Romantic movement in Germany.

Schopenhauer, Arthur (1778–1860): German philosopher and essayist who combined Immanuel Kant with Indian philosophy.

Shankara, also called Adi Shankaracharya (ca. 700–750): Indian philosopher in the Advaita Vedanta school who wrote about the self and knowledge.

Smith, Adam (1723–1790): Scottish economist who wrote *The Wealth of Nations* and *The Theory of Moral Sentiments*.

Socrates (ca. 470–399 BCE): Athenian philosopher credited as the founder of Western philosophy who preached mostly about ethics.

Sophocles (497–406 BCE): Greek playwright who wrote *Oedipus, Antigone,* and other tragedies.

Spinoza, Baruch (1632–1677): Dutch (and Portuguese Jewish) philosopher who wrote about ethics, metaphysics, and biblical criticism.

Strawson, Galen (1952–): British philosopher and literary critic who focuses on philosophy of mind, metaphysics, and epistemology.

Strawson, Peter Frederick (1919–2006): English philosopher who wrote about language, free will, and metaphysics.

Sunzi, also called Sun Tzu (ca. 544–496 BCE): Chinese general believed to have authored *The Art of War.*

Thales of Miletus (ca. 626–548 BCE): Pre-Socratic Greek mathematician and astronomer born in Turkey who said everything is water.

Thomas Aquinas, Saint
(1225-1274): Italian priest
who combined Aristotle
with Christianity in writing about theology and
metaphysics.

Turing, Alan (1912-1954):
English mathematician
and logician who invented
the first computer, called a
Turing machine.

Vatsyayana (ca. 2nd or
3rd century CE): Indian
philosopher who pro-
vided commentary on the
Nyaya-sutras.

Vyasa, also called Krishna
Dvaipayana: Legendary
sage cited as the author
of the Hindu epic
Mahabharata, including the
Bhagavad Gita.

Warhol, Andy (1928-1987):
American artist and
film director who said
that everyone will have
15 minutes of fame.

**Whitehead, Alfred
North** (1861-1947): English
mathematician and
philosopher who developed
process philosophy.

William of Occam, sometimes spelled Ockham
(1285-1347): English clergyman who invented the
principle of Occam's razor
and wrote about metaphys-
ics, logic, and theology.

Williams, Bernard (1929-
2003): English moral
philosopher who demanded
that philosophy deal with
the complexity of human life.

Wittgenstein, Ludwig
(1889-1951): Austrian
British philosopher who
wrote about logic, mathe-
matics, and the philosophy
of mind and language.

**Wolff, Christian Freiherr
von** (1679-1754): German
philosopher who wrote on
all topics, especially mathematics and aesthetics.

**Wright, Georg Henrik
von** (1916-2003): Finnish
philosopher who wrote
about modal logic, language,
and mind.

Wu Boli (ca. 1400): Chinese
Daoist priest and artist at
the Shangqing temple on
Dragon Tiger Mountain.

Glossary

ad hominem fallacy: attacking the opponent in an argument instead of the opponent's position

aesthetics: the study of the appreciation of beauty

argument: one or more reasons (premises) presented to convince someone of a conclusion

axiom: a basic rule of a system accepted as true and used to deduce other sentences that will be true for that system

causality: when one event produces another

coherence theory of truth: a theory that says a belief is true if it fits (coheres) with other beliefs

correlation: when two things tend to appear or move together

deductive argument: an argument where the truth of the premise logically implies the truth of the conclusion

democracy: a system of government where laws are decided by popular vote

determinism: the idea that all events are caused by prior events, which implies that human actions aren't the result of free choices

dialogue: a story that's written like a play, where two or more people are having a conversation

dualism: i.e., mind-body dualism; the idea that mind and body are fundamentally different kinds of substance and that these are the only two kinds of substance that exist

egalitarianism: the idea that all people are equal

ego: one's sense of self-importance

empiricism: the idea that all knowledge comes ultimately from the senses

epistemology: the study of how we know things

equivocation: when an argument uses two different meanings of a word as if they were the same

essence: the quality of something that makes it what it is, without which it wouldn't be that thing

essentialism: the idea that things have essences

ethics: the study of moral principles, which are standards for correct behavior

existentialism: a philosophy that says that human choices are totally free, both from prior causes like an essential human nature and from reasons that would force us to make particular choices

faith: belief in something or someone that does not require reasons

functionalism: the idea in the philosophy of mind that mental states such as beliefs and desires are just functions the mind performs

hermeneutics: the branch of knowledge that deals with interpretation

idealism: the metaphysical position that everything is just ideas

induction: using a number of instances of something to argue for a universal claim (for example: "I've seen one hundred white swans and none of any other color, therefore all swans are white")

informal fallacies: bad arguments in natural language, as opposed to formal logical systems

integrity: when things (like parts of a human life) fit together; in ethics, this refers to moral correctness, with the idea that doing the right thing is a matter of not lying or otherwise dividing your words from your actions

karma: the idea in Hinduism and Buddhism that your actions generate moral residue that determines your fate, in particular what you will be in your next life

logic: the study of argument forms and how some statements logically imply others

Machiavellian: ruthless in political matters

materialist: the metaphysical idea that everything is made of matter

metaphysics: the study of what reality ultimately is

modus ponens: a rule in logic: 1. If P is true then Q is true; 2. P is true; 3. Therefore Q is true

modus tollens: a rule in logic: 1. If P is true, then Q is true; 2. Q is false; 3. Therefore, P is false

morality: a system of values expressing what's right and wrong (often refers to one's personal code, as opposed to ethics, which can refer to a shared code, though the words are often used interchangeably)

negation: the contradiction or denial of something

negative theology: saying what God is not rather than what God is

normative: a claim that involves a value judgment; a claim that you should do something

noumenal world: for Immanuel Kant, the world as it is in itself, apart from human knowers

ontology: part of metaphysics; a list of types of things that exist

paradigm: in general, a model or standard case of something; for Thomas Kuhn, a set of standards for conducting science and what counts as a legitimate scientific finding

phenomenal world: for Immanuel Kant, the world as it appears to us

Platonic Forms: in Plato's philosophy, perfect ideas that the things we perceive in the world are modeled after

politics: activities that people engage in to govern, which are studied by political philosophy

pragmatic theory of truth: a theory that defines a belief as true insofar as it can be used to act successfully

predicate logic: a way of extending propositional logic that allows for predicates to be symbolized and applied to individual things (for example, "The dog is furry" could be symbolized as Fd, while "The cat is furry" would be Fc)

premise: a reason given in a logical argument that is supposed to provide support for a conclusion

quantifier: a concept used to say that a predicate applies to some set of objects (for example, the "all" in "All dogs are furry")

rationalism: the idea that all knowledge comes ultimately from reason

reason: the human ability to gain knowledge from abstract concepts

reductio ad absurdum: proving that a premise is false by showing that it has absurd (self-contradictory) logical consequences

reductionism: in metaphysics, the idea that something can be redescribed in more basic terms (for example, a reductionist about minds thinks that mind is not a basic ontological category, but can instead be redescribed in materialist or other terms)

refute: to successfully argue against

Romanticism: an intellectual and artistic movement in Europe toward the end of the 18th century that stressed feeling over reason

self: one's own existence as an individual

self-evident: accepted as obviously true without requiring any reasons

skepticism: doubt about some or all knowledge

slippery slope: a claim that some action, even though it's not terrible by itself, will inevitably lead to worse future actions

social construction: the idea that something has been created merely by agreement between people

social contract: an implicit (unstated) agreement between people to live together in society under rules

social justice: each person receiving whatever is morally due to them in a political situation

soul: the spiritual, immaterial part of a person (for many philosophers, this is the mind)

straw man: attacking a position that is not actually the one your opponent holds

sublime: arousing fear for aesthetic effect, typically through something's enormous size and power

syllogism: a structure that presents valid reasoning

utilitarianism: the idea that what's best is what benefits the most and hurts the least

virtue: a morally good character trait

Will: for Arthur Schopenhauer, the irrational inner essence of the world

Resources

The best way to learn more about the ideas in this book is to just do some web research. If there's a particular philosopher that sounds interesting to you, you can look up that author's most famous book, and give it a try!

WEBSITES

Internet Encyclopedia of Philosophy: iep.utm.edu

The Stanford Encyclopedia of Philosophy: plato .stanford.edu

History of Philosophy Without Any Gaps (podcast): historyofphilosophy.net

The Partially Examined Life (podcast): partiallyexaminedlife .com

Philosophize This! (podcast): philosophizethis.org

BIBLIOGRAPHY

Barker, Stephen F. *The Elements of Logic*. McGraw-Hill, 1989.

Bonevac, Daniel & Phillips, Stephen. *Understanding Non-Western Philosophy*. Mayfield, 1993.

Christian, James L. *Philosophy: An Introduction to the Art of Wondering*. Cengage Learning, 2011.

Melchert, Norman. *The Great Conversation: A Historical Introduction to Philosophy*. McGraw-Hill, 2018.

Palmer, Donald. *Does the Center Hold? An Introduction to Western Philosophy*. McGraw-Hill, 2020.

Patton, Michael F. *The Cartoon Introduction to Philosophy*. Hill and Wang, 2015.

The Philosophy Book: Big Ideas Simply Explained. DK, 2017.

Pojman, Louis P. *The Moral Life: An Introductory Reader in Ethics and Literature*. Oxford University Press, 2017.

Van Lente, Fred. *Action Philosophers*. Dark Horse Books, 2014.

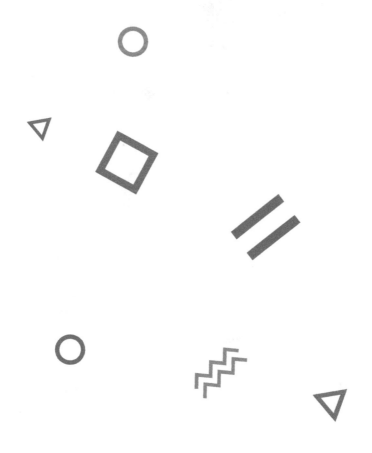

Index

ACKNOWLEDGMENTS

The questions and figures chosen for this book emerged from my understanding garnered from numerous teachers at the University of Michigan, Ann Arbor, and the University of Texas at Austin, plus hundreds of discussions with my *Partially Examined Life* cohosts Wes Alwan, Seth Paskin, and Dylan Casey, and our guests.

A book like this leaves no room to cite all the web sources used to ascertain or confirm details about these authors' views, so thank you to the cloud, and any errors in compiling its wisdom are mine.

ABOUT THE AUTHOR

Mark Linsenmayer grew up in the Chicago area, the son of a folk singer and a nurse. He spent far too many years in school, earning an MA and MLIS and all the requirements for a PhD apart from that pesky dissertation. After 2000, he worked in technical communications while occasionally teaching philosophy. He started *The Partially Examined Life* podcast in 2009 and now runs four podcasts. He blogs frequently about philosophy and music; this is his second book. He is married with two college-age children and lives in Madison, Wisconsin. For more information, see marklint.com and partiallyexaminedlife.com.